99 **Earth-Shattering Events**
Linked to the Bible

B

museum of the Bible

BOOKS

Executive Editorial Team
Allen Quine
Wayne Hastings
Jeana Ledbetter
Byron Williamson

Managing Editor
Christopher D. Hudson

**Developmental
Editorial Team**
Tricia Drevets
Peggy Harvey
Andrew Klosterman
Brent McCulley
Laurence Paul
Melissa Peitsch
Daniel Reeves
Brad Spencer
Paula Stiles
Jennifer Turner
Len Woods

Worthy Editorial
Kyle Olund
Leeanna Nelson

Design & Page Layout
Mark Wainwright,
Symbology Creative

Cover Design
Matt Smartt,
Smartt Guys design

99 Earth-Shattering Events Linked to the Bible
© 2017 Museum of the Bible, Inc., Washington, DC 20014
Published by Worthy Publishing Group, a division of Worthy Media, Inc. in association with Museum of the Bible.

ISBN-10: 1945470089
ISBN-13: 978-1945470080

Library of Congress number for 99 Events: 2017947427

Unless otherwise indicated, Scripture quotations are from the ESV® Bible (The Holy Bible, English Standard Version®), copyright © 2001 by Crossway, a publishing ministry of Good News Publishers. Used by permission. All rights reserved.

Scripture quotations marked KJV are taken from The Holy Bible, King James Version. Public Domain.

Scripture quotations marked NKJV are taken from the New King James Version®.
Copyright © 1982 by Thomas Nelson. Used by permission. All rights reserved.

Produced with the assistance of Hudson Bible.

Printed in the USA

1 2 3 4 5 6 7 8 9 LAKE 22 21 20 19 18 17

Cover image: Reprinted by arrangement with The Heirs to the Estate of Martin Luther King Jr., c/o Writer's House as agent for the proprietor New York, NY.
Lightstock: 9,73
Art Resource: 26
Istockphoto: 12, 31, 53, 61, 91, 93
Shutterstock: 6, 8, 10, 11, 13, 14, 15, 16, 17, 18, 19, 20, 21, 23, 28, 29, 30, 34, 37, 38, 40, 41, 42, 44, 45, 47, 48, 49, 52, 54, 55, 56, 59, 62, 63, 64, 65, 67, 68, 69, 70, 71, 72, 74, 75, 76, 77, 78, 79, 80, 81, 82, 83, 85, 86, 87, 88, 92, 94, 95, 96, 98, 100, 101, 102, 103, 104, 105, 106, 107, 108, 109
All other images from Commons.Wikimedia.org

museum of the Bible
BOOKS

WORTHY®
PUBLISHING

Introduction 5

01   The Maccabean Revolt Is the First Religious War 7
02   Constantine Issues the Edict of Milan 8
03   Basil of Caesarea Promotes Social Justice 9
04   Telemachus's Stand Abolishes Gladiatorial Games 10
05   Boethius Writes The Consolation of Philosophy 11
06   Dionysius Exiguus Calculates Years by Anno Domini 12
07   The Justinian Code Revolutionizes Roman Law 13
08   Bede Becomes the Father of English History 14
09   Alfred the Great Reforms English Society 15
10   Vladimir Adopts Christianity 16
11   Maimonides Creates the Mishneh Torah 17
12   Francis of Assisi Founds the Franciscan Order 18
13   The Magna Carta Sets a Standard for Law 20
14   Chartres Cathedral Is Consecrated 21
15   Thomas Aquinas Clarifies Christian Theology in Summa Theologica 22
16   Petrarch Helps Launch the Renaissance 23
17   John Ball Emboldens the Peasants' Revolt 24
18   Joan of Arc Leads France in Battle 25
19   Johannes Gutenberg Prints the First Bible 26
20   Leonardo da Vinci Paints The Last Supper 27
21   Michelangelo Carves the World's Greatest Statue 28
22   Michelangelo's Sistine Chapel Illustrates Biblical Creation 29
23   Martin Luther Launches the Protestant Reformation 30
24   Ferdinand Magellan Sails to Spread Christianity 31
25   William Tyndale's English Translation Impacts Society 32
26   Nicolaus Copernicus Reveals an Orderly Creator 34
27   Tycho Brahe Revolutionizes Astronomy 35
28   Francis Bacon Develops the Scientific Method 36
29   Johannes Kepler Originates Intelligent Design 37
30   Miguel de Cervantes Writes the First Modern Novel 38
31   John Rolfe Promotes Christianity in the New World 39
32   Galileo Seeks to Harmonize Religion and Science 40
33   The King James Bible Is Published 41
34   The Pilgrims Seek Religious Freedom in the New World 42
35   Massachusetts Founds Harvard University to Train Clergy 43
36   René Descartes Sets Foundation for Modern Philosophy 44
37   Blaise Pascal Integrates Reason and Faith 45
38   Rembrandt Finds Inspiration in Biblical Stories 46
39   John Flamsteed Opposes Agnostic Astronomers 47
40   Gottfried Leibniz Discovers Calculus 48
41   Robert Boyle Endeavors to Spread Christianity 49
42   William Penn Founds Pennsylvania as a "Holy Experiment" 50
43   Isaac Newton Makes Scientific Breakthroughs 51
44   John Locke Creates the Social Contract Theory 52

45 The English Bill of Rights Guarantees Freedom...53

46 American Classrooms Use the Bible as a Primary Text...54

47 Johann Sebastian Bach Composes Beloved Worship Music..55

48 George Frideric Handel's Messiah Celebrates the Life of Jesus....................................56

49 Antoine Lavoisier Helps Invent Modern Chemistry...57

50 John Witherspoon Protects Religious Liberty..58

51 Adam Smith Originates Modern Economic Theory..59

52 Robert Raikes's Sunday School Movement Reaches Orphans......................................60

53 Immanuel Kant Transforms Philosophical Study...62

54 William Wilberforce Opposes British Slave Trade...63

55 Former Slave Exposes Horror of Slavery..64

56 George Washington Becomes the First US President...65

57 Benjamin Rush Champions Nationalized School System..66

58 James Madison Promotes Freedom of Religion in the US Bill of Rights.......................67

59 William Carey Influences the Indian Renaissance...68

60 John Dalton Founds Modern Atomic Theory...69

61 Alessandro Volta Invents the First Battery...70

62 Elizabeth Fry Initiates Prison Reform...71

63 Michael Faraday Contributes to Electromagnetism and Electrochemistry....................72

64 Lord Shaftesbury Enacts Social Reforms..73

65 André-Marie Ampère Pioneers Electrodynamics..74

66 The Second Great Awakening Reshapes a Nation...75

67 George Mueller Cares for Abandoned Children...76

68 John Quincy Adams Wins Freedom for African Slaves in the Amistad Supreme Court Case...77

69 Samuel Morse's First Telegraph Message Acknowledges God.......................................78

70 Frederick Douglass Works to Abolish Slavery...79

71 Charles Dickens Inspires Social Reform...80

72 Lord Kelvin Develops Laws of Thermodynamics...81

73 Louis Pasteur Investigates Germs and Invents Life-Saving Vaccines..........................82

74 Clara Barton Founds the Red Cross...83

75 Victor Hugo Draws on Biblical Themes in His Writings..84

76 Abraham Lincoln Signs the Emancipation Proclamation...85

77 "In God We Trust" Added to US Coins and Paper Currency..86

78 William Booth Founds the Salvation Army to Assist the Poor.......................................87

79 John D. Rockefeller Establishes Faith-Based Philanthropy..88

80 Guglielmo Marconi Develops the Radio Telegraph System...89

81 Oxyrhynchus Papyri Are Discovered in Egypt..90

82 Amy Carmichael Rescues Girls and Women in India..90

83 Henri Dunant Receives the First Nobel Peace Prize...92

84 Albert Schweitzer Treats the Sick and Preaches the Bible in Africa............................93

85 Woodrow Wilson Creates the Fourteen Points of Peace...94

86 George Washington Carver Unlocks Peanut's Potential...95

87 Dorothy Day Cofounds the Catholic Worker Movement..96

88 Chiune Sugihara Saves Jews during World War II...97

89 Winston Churchill Leads Britain to Join the Allied Forces...98

90 Bedouin Shepherds Discover the Dead Sea Scrolls 100
91 Jews Gather in Jerusalem to Celebrate Their First Passover in Modern Israel 101
92 Mother Teresa Founds the Missionaries of Charity 102
93 Frank País Attempts Overthrow of Batista 103
94 Christian UN Chief Champions the Underdog 104
95 Martin Luther King Jr. Leads Civil Rights Movement 105
96 Gary Starkweather Invents the Laser Printer 106
97 Neil Armstrong Walks on the Moon 107
98 Nelson Mandela Negotiates to End Apartheid 108
99 Paul Rusesabagina Saves Hundreds During the Rwandan Genocide 110

References 111
About the Museum of the Bible 112

99 Earth-Shattering Events Linked to the Bible

Introduction

Throughout history the Bible has dramatically influenced the thinking and actions of people around the world. In this book, readers will find ninety-nine examples of how the Bible has inspired men and women to bring improvements to our world. Motivated by the Bible, some lost their lives to stand against injustice. Others started and sustained charitable efforts to bring relief to the poor and destitute. Still others revolutionized science and technology.

Surprising connections between the Bible and significant events of our world are discussed while also providing a full-color opportunity for readers to explore some of the most monumental events and people in history. Those interested in deepening their knowledge of the Bible and those who love history will enjoy reading this book.

Perhaps the events and people in this book will also inspire us to continue improving the world for the benefit of future generations.

(01

The Maccabean Revolt Is the First Religious War

When Antiochus IV Epiphanes became the ruler of the Seleucid Empire in 175 BC, he issued a decree that made possessing the Hebrew Bible an offense punishable by death, and he burned all the copies of the Bible that he was able to find. He also banned many Jewish practices, including circumcising males, observing the Sabbath and the feasts, and offering sacrifices. He further demanded that Jews forsake their worship of the God of Israel and instead worship foreign gods—or be put to death.

If Antiochus's attempt to eradicate the Hebrew Bible and religious practices had succeeded, it's possible that Judaism would have ceased to exist. And without the Bible, Christianity and Islam would not exist in the forms we know them today either.

However, Antiochus made a costly mistake. He underestimated the Jews' devotion to their God and his laws. Instead of submitting to the emperor's orders to worship false gods, the Jews held firmly to the Bible's commands to worship God alone. They took seriously the commandment in Exodus 20:3, 5: "You shall have no other gods before me. . . . You shall not bow down to them or serve them, for I the LORD your God am a jealous God."

Taking these words to heart, the Jews did not waver. When Antiochus's troops demanded that the Jews sacrifice a pig to the Greek gods, a Jewish leader named Mattathias refused. Mattathias and his family fled to the hills and assembled an army of faithful Jews, led by his son Judah, who was nicknamed Maccabee ("The Hammer"). This guerilla army, known as the Maccabees, mounted a revolt against Antiochus. Their resistance to religious persecution led many Jews to death, as they preferred to die as martyrs rather than forsake their God and transgress his laws as expressed in the Bible.

The Maccabean Revolt set a historical precedent as the first religious war. In the ancient world people didn't die for their gods; only the Jews considered their God worth dying for.

After a hard-fought victory over the Seleucids, the Maccabees entered Jerusalem in triumph and rededicated the temple. The Jewish festival of Hanukkah (meaning "to dedicate") celebrates this significant event. ∎

Left: The Hebrew Torah, displayed here on a synagogue altar, is handwritten on goat skin parchment by a specially trained scribe using a feather quill.

02 Constantine Issues the Edict of Milan

In the third century AD, authorities of the Roman Empire called for all biblical manuscripts to be burned in order to crush the growing Christian movement. While many early Christians interpreted their sacred texts as commanding them to obey worldly authorities, the Romans felt that Christians were subversive and dangerous. Christians' refusal to worship the Roman emperor was seen as disloyal if not treasonous.

These Christians faced an agonizing decision. Should they hand over copies of their biblical texts to the pagan authorities and be shunned by other Christians as *traditores*? (This word, Latin for "handers-over," is the source of our English word *traitor*.) Or should they resist and face the certainty of persecution and possibly death?

Everything changed in AD 313 when Constantine the Great signed the Edict of Milan.

Constantine was the first Roman emperor to profess Christianity. In order to restore privileges and property to Christians who had suffered under the Great Persecution, Constantine signed the Edict of Milan, which legalized Christianity and granted full religious freedom to Christians. As a result of this edict, Christians could gather openly and worship without fear of persecution.

Constantine also provided resources to replace copies of biblical texts that had been destroyed during the years of persecution under previous Roman emperors. Constantine enlisted the help of Eusebius, a Greek historian and biblical scholar, to prepare fifty copies of the Bible for the churches in Constantinople. Additionally, he instituted restrictions on the branding of prisoners' faces, as this was now to be considered contrary to the Bible's teaching that humankind was created in the image of God (Genesis 1:27).

Constantine's Edict of Milan helped Christianity become a widely accepted faith. Therefore, it was more easily spread throughout the world, bringing with it a high regard for humanity. By the fourth century AD, Christianity had become the dominant religion in the Roman Empire. ■

Top: *The Torches of Nero* by Henryk Siemiradzki (1843–1902).
Top Right: Sculpted head of Emperor Constantine.
Left: Mosaic of Emperor Constantine in the Hagia Sophia, Istanbul, Turkey.

03 Basil of Caesarea Promotes Social Justice

Various biblical texts support strong protection of the most vulnerable or marginalized members of society, such as orphans, widows, and the poor. Early Christian texts advocate a degree of equality that was exceptional for its time and place.

St. Basil was a bishop in Caesarea whose study of the Bible inspired him to seek justice in a society that was profiting off the poor. He not only showed genuine care and compassion to those in need but also rejected some of the common, unbiblical practices of his era. One of these practices was usury, the practice of lending money to people in desperate financial situations at unreasonably high interest rates. While usury appeared to lift the poor out of their misery, in reality it took advantage of those who were suffering from poverty.

According to the Bible, this is not what God intended. Proverbs 28:8 says, "One who increases his possessions by usury and extortion gathers it for him who will pity the poor" (NKJV).

As bishop of Caesarea, St. Basil used the Bible and his own influence to realign the focus of the society he lived in to more closely resemble the values found in the Bible.

Always compassionate to those who needed assistance, St. Basil sold all his possessions and used them to help the poor and underprivileged. He is remembered as the first bishop to establish hospitals, orphanages, and homes for the elderly. Even though he died at only forty-nine years old, he is regarded as one of the greatest fathers of the church. ∎

04 Telemachus's Stand Abolishes Gladiatorial Games

When Telemachus, a Christian monk, traveled to Rome in the early fifth century, he could not have anticipated the lasting influence of his actions. While in Rome, Telemachus witnessed the gruesome acts of the gladiators battling in the arena. He was deeply disturbed by this premeditated and unnecessary killing, which was in defiance of the sixth commandment listed in the Ten Commandments: "You shall not murder" (Exodus 20:13).

Horrified as he watched the gladiators killing one another for the crowd's entertainment, Telemachus rushed into the arena to stop what he knew the Bible said was wrong. According to *Foxe's Book of Martyrs*, Telemachus tried to convince the fighters of the cruelty of their actions. He stood between the gladiators and begged them to stop, crying, "Do not requite God's mercy in turning away the swords of your enemies by murdering each other!"

The crowds that had gathered for the event went into an uproar. They wanted to be entertained by the gladiators' bloody battle, not to have this unwelcomed interruption by a humble, robed monk. Their response was swift and harsh. The furious crowd hurled down stones and killed Telemachus for disturbing the event.

Telemachus's bold stand in the Colosseum that day was an act that changed history. Inspired by Telemachus's sacrificial act to preserve life, Emperor Honorius abolished the gladiatorial games three days later. No gladiator ever fought to the death in the Colosseum again. ■

Top: The Roman Colosseum, Rome, Italy.

05 Boethius Writes
The Consolation of Philosophy

As a philosopher and Roman government officer, Anicius Manlius Severinus Boethius translated Greek philosophy and classic literature into Latin. His most famous contribution is *The Consolation of Philosophy*, which he wrote while in prison for treason. It became one of the most widely read and influential works of the Middle Ages.

The Consolation is the story of Boethius, who imagines he is visited by Lady Philosophy. Their discussions cover numerous philosophical topics, such as happiness, fortune, fame, virtue, justice, evil, and death. In this book Boethius reveals there is a higher power, explains that all human suffering has a higher purpose, and outlines how people can achieve balance between happiness and fortune.

The Consolation has been described as having the single most important influence on Christianity during the Middle Ages and early Renaissance, and it has been hailed as the last great work of the classical period.

While this significant literary work does not mention any specific religion, Boethius did refer to biblical concepts throughout his writing. ■

Left: Relief depicting Narius Manlius Boethius, father of the famous author Anicius Manlius Severinus Boethius.
Above: Parthenon, Athens, Greece.

11

06 Dionysius Exiguus Calculates Years by Anno Domini

The widely used term *Anno Domini*—abbreviated AD—is Latin for "in the year of our Lord." Today, the worldwide use of AD to calculate years shows the tremendous influence of the teachings of the Bible.

Dionysius Exiguus of Scythia Minor, a Christian monk who lived in Rome, introduced the AD system in the year 525 as a way to count the years since the birth of Jesus. Before Dionysius, Romans had counted years *ab urbe condita*, or "from the founding of the city."

The AD system was not used on a broad basis until the ninth century when Charlemagne proclaimed it official for the Holy Roman Empire. England began using the system by the twelfth century, and as England's colonization spread, so did the use of AD.

In 1582, Pope Gregory XIII made a few changes to the Julian calendar (named for Julius Caesar), primarily so that Easter could be celebrated at the right astronomical time. The Gregorian calendar—and the use of AD—then became firmly established in Spain and France and other Roman Catholic countries. As international trade spread, the use of AD reached much of the rest of the world and forever transformed how much of the world calculates time and history. ◾

Above: Mosaic of Jesus Christ, Istanbul, Turkey.

07 The Justinian Code Revolutionizes Roman Law

Roman emperor Justinian was notorious for his abuses of power and mistreatment of Jews and other non-Christians under his rule. Yet he is also remembered positively for his contribution to jurisprudence (the study of the philosophies and theories of law).

In the late fifth century, and well into the sixth, Emperor Justinian was focused on restoring an ailing empire that had been weakened by military fighting and religious disagreement. Previous emperors had issued decrees that contradicted Roman law, leaving Justinian to inherit a confused jumble of Roman laws that had accumulated over about a thousand years, including laws that contradicted each other. It was difficult to keep the laws updated in the various parts of the empire. So to clear up any confusion and make it easier to administer justice across the empire, Justinian convened a commission of leading legal minds to develop a more consistent and cohesive legal code.

The resulting *Codex Constitutionum*, written in 529, became the law of the land, together with two other legal compendiums issued around 532–534. Historians now refer to the commission's legal summations as the Justinian Code. This enshrined many biblical principles and teachings and also originated the solemn practice of swearing on the Bible.

> *"To know the laws means not to accept the words, but their meaning and significance."*
> – Justinian

The Bible greatly influenced Justinian's reforms regarding social injustices. The Justinian Code outlawed child abandonment, child slavery, and infanticide, which were all norms during his reign. Justinian resisted these practices based on biblical principles of the God-given value of human life.

The Justinian Code had a major influence on public law across Europe. Many historians agree that Justinian's Code, despite some defects, became the basis for many of Europe's legal systems. The Justinian Code is considered the foundation of Western legal tradition, and it forms the basis of modern civil law. All the legal systems throughout the West still use the Justinian Code as a philosophical basis, including those in Africa, Europe, and Latin America. ■

Left: Mosaic of Emperor Justinian. Basilica of San Vitale, Ravenna, Italy.

08

Bede Becomes the Father of English History

Bede, an English monk, scholar, linguist, and translator authored more than forty books about many areas of knowledge, including mathematics, astronomy, history, theology, grammar, nature, astronomy, and poetry. His most famous work is *The Ecclesiastical History of the English People*, a significant accomplishment that made him known as the father of English history.

Written around 731, Bede's five-volume work is the first comprehensive history ever written of the early English Christian church, as well as English secular life. Without Bede's *Ecclesiastical History*, we would not have any reliable history of Anglo-Saxon England before the Dark Ages. His book remains the single most valuable source for this period. Bede provides important insights into the civic and religious growth of England, as well as details about major historical events such as Julius Caesar's invasion in 55 BC, the reigns of Northumbrian kings Oswald and Oswy, and the Council of Whitby, which were all major turning points in English history.

In *Ecclesiastical History*, Bede—often called "Venerable Bede" because of his pious devotion to God—tells how Christianity spread throughout England. In the New Testament, Jesus gives a final command to his followers: "Go therefore and make disciples of all nations" (Matthew 28:19). In his book, Bede recounts the ways that several notable people followed this command, including Augustine, who brought Christianity to England; Theodore, who was consecrated as the Archbishop of Canterbury; and Wilfrid, who worked to convert the Sussex kingdom.

Bede's meticulous documentation of religious historical events gives us a more complete understanding of the Bible's influence on world history. ■

Hadrian's Wall, Northumberland, England.

09 Alfred the Great Reforms English Society

King Alfred—the first English king to be given the designation "the Great"—is considered to be one of the most extraordinary kings in English history.

King Alfred put into practice many of the Bible's teachings during his nearly thirty-year reign. He saw himself as the defender of all Christian Anglo-Saxons against the pagan Vikings, and he worked to free neighboring areas from Viking control. He made peace with the Danes after years of conflict and encouraged the people of England to pursue education.

Alfred was greatly influenced by the Bible, and he used his authority as a means for the betterment of the land. The most obvious biblical impact of Alfred's reign is found in his legal code. King Alfred's laws implemented instructions from the Hebrew Bible books of Moses, such as the sixth commandment: "Thou shalt not kill" (Exodus 20:13, KJV). In comparison, Alfred's law reads, "A just and innocent man, him slay thou never."[1] His laws also reflect the New Testament's teachings about treating members of different socioeconomic classes as equal (James 2:1–13). Through King Alfred's laws, the Bible's teachings helped to shape English society. ■

Above: King Alfred the Great statue erected in 1899 stands at the eastern end of the Broadway in Winchester Hampshire, England.
A coin of Alfred, king of Wessex, London, 880.

10 Vladimir Adopts Christianity

By the tenth century, Christianity had found its way to Russia. Tribes who immigrated to Russia from Scandinavia brought their religious heritage with them, and Greek missionaries—such as Constantine, who was later named Cyril, and Methodios (ca. 815–885)—shared their faith with many Russians.

Historians know that at least one church was built in the ancient city of Kiev in the 950s. However, it was not until the reign of Vladimir I, prince of Kiev, that Christianity became Russia's official religion.

Vladimir, who reigned from 980 to 1015, saw religion as a unifying factor for his vast nation. Although he built several pagan temples early in his reign and lived a fast lifestyle, he was influenced by his Christian grandmother, Olga, who had been baptized.

The monarch sent emissaries to other parts of the world to bring him information on the religions of the world, including Orthodox Christianity of the Byzantine Empire. He was especially impressed by reports of the dazzling cathedral of Hagia Sophia in Constantinople.

In 988, Vladimir selected Orthodox Christianity for his country, and he invited priests, architects, and icon painters from the Byzantine Empire to Russia to help with the conversion process.

By following the teaching of the Bible, Vladimir radically changed his own lifestyle. He was baptized and had a Christian marriage ceremony with his wife, Anne. He gave the church judicial powers in family law and moral matters.

He also built churches, distributed food and clothes to the needy, and even invited the poor to share banquet tables with him. Vladimir also designated 10% of state income for the church. ∎

Above: Copper bas-relief of Prince Vladimir, Cathedral of the Blessed Virgin Mary, Kiev.
Left: Saint Andrew's Church, Kiev.

11 Maimonides Creates the Mishneh Torah

The *Mishneh Torah* ranks among the greatest and most innovative Jewish legal texts of all time. It has had profound influence throughout the history of Jewish faith and still influences how many people within the Jewish faith interpret the Bible.

Aside from being revered by Jewish scholars and historians, Maimonides also influenced prominent Muslim and Christian philosophers, and even scholars such as Averroës and Thomas Aquinas. He is remembered today as much for his humane character as for his exceptional breadth of learning and wisdom. ■

Maimonides was a Jewish physician, scientist, and scholar. His Hebrew name was Rabbi Moses ben Maimon, though many Jews refer to him using the acronym of his name: Rambam. Considered one of the greatest thinkers of all time, this twelfth-century Jewish sage is acknowledged as one of the foremost rabbinical scholars and philosophers in Jewish history.

Maimonides was born in Spain around 1135, but he fled persecution with his family to Morocco, later to Israel, and finally to Egypt. There he produced his great philosophic work *The Guide for the Perplexed*, wrote numerous books on medicine, served as physician to the sultan of Egypt, and became the leader of the Jewish community in Cairo.

Maimonides described eight levels of charitable giving (*tzedakah*) in a treatise called "The Golden Ladder of Tzedakah." For Maimonides, the highest form of charity was to help a person become self-reliant, if possible, so that he or she would have no need for assistance.

Maimonides's major contribution to Jewish life was his codification of Jewish law, which he called *Mishneh Torah* ("repetition of the Torah"). The fourteen-volume work guides Jews on how to behave in all situations, without having to expend large amounts of time searching through the Talmud (the central text of rabbinical Judaism) for the laws of Shabbat, holidays, prayer, dietary laws, and the laws that regulate daily Jewish life.

Above: Jewish man prays at Maimonides's tomb in Tiberias, Israel.
Right: Statue of Ben Maimonides in the Jewish Quarter of Córdoba, Spain.

12 Francis of Assisi Founds the Franciscan Order

Born Francesco di Bernardone, the man we know as St. Francis of Assisi was the son of a wealthy cloth merchant from Spoleto, Italy. He was educated, knowing Latin and also some French. He was a natural leader who easily engaged people. As a young man, he lived a carefree, worldly life in medieval Italian society.

But when Francis went through the difficult experience of being a prisoner of war, the trajectory of his life changed. His imprisonment had a profound effect on him, and he experienced dreams and visions that convinced him that the Bible was to be known, preached, and lived. He began to sell off his family fortune to raise money for the church.

Against his father's wishes, Francis left home and began to live as a hermit. Inspired by the Bible's teachings, he established the Franciscans, a Christian religious order centered on poverty and self-sacrifice. The First Order of Franciscans started as a small band of twelve men, but it soon became very popular and grew rapidly in number.

> *"Where there is injury let me sow pardon."* – Francis of Assisi

The Franciscans preached the gospel, aided the poor, and tended to those in need. Francis also established an order for women called the Order of Saint Clare (also known as the Poor Clares). Like the Franciscans, the members of this order were committed to living out the commands of the Bible by serving those who lived in poverty and being charitable with their time and efforts.

The Franciscans traveled to France, Spain, Germany, England, Hungary, and Turkey, preaching their message of repentance, simplicity, and obedience to Jesus's teaching. Their teaching and example sparked a religious revival that spread all over Europe. Francis's life was so remarkable and clearly committed to God that he was canonized as a saint only two years after his death—exceptionally fast by Roman Catholic standards.

St. Francis of Assisi, Croatian Academy of Sciences, Zagreb, Croatia.

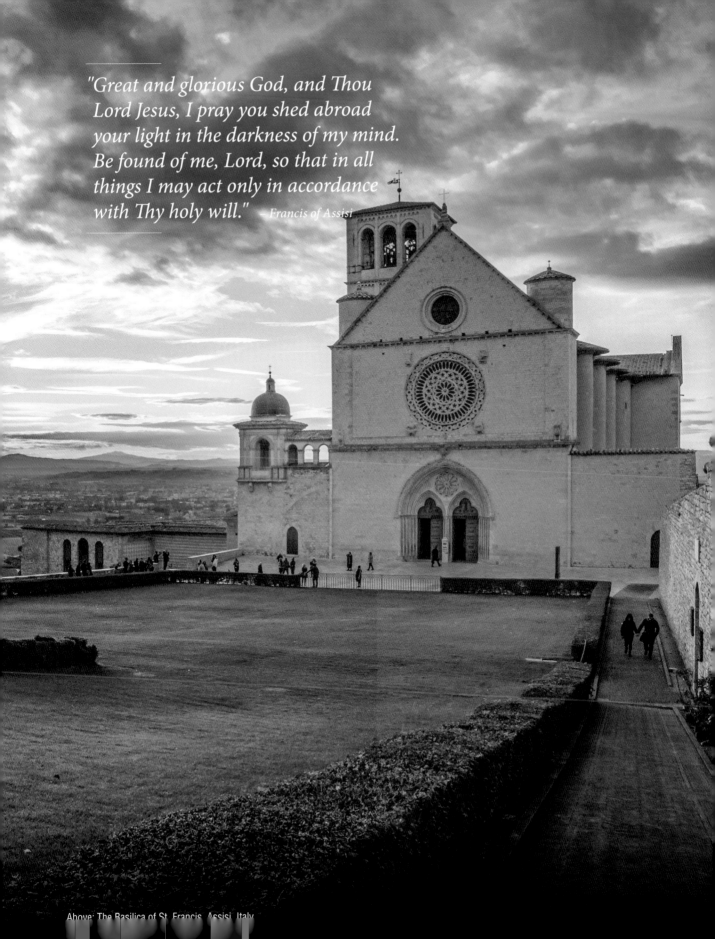

"Great and glorious God, and Thou Lord Jesus, I pray you shed abroad your light in the darkness of my mind. Be found of me, Lord, so that in all things I may act only in accordance with Thy holy will." — Francis of Assisi

Above: The Basilica of St. Francis, Assisi, Italy

13 The Magna Carta Sets a Standard for Law

As legal systems became more sophisticated in England, the relationship between the rulers and the ruled also changed.

King John ruled England during the early thirteenth century. Pressured by church officials and English barons to limit his own power, King John signed the Magna Carta (Latin for "Great Charter"), a landmark document that declared for the first time in history that kings were not above the law but subject to it.

The Magna Carta declared what its formulators expected of the king and his subjects regarding civil liberties. In time, the power of the king was further curtailed by the rise of Parliament. The king could not raise taxes or pass new laws without the consent of Parliament. The judiciary was given the task of interpreting and enforcing the law, effectively acting independently of the king.

The Magna Carta was a source of inspiration in the development of modern systems of government. The founding documents of the individual colonies and states in the United States reflect the Magna Carta's view that even rulers are held accountable to justice. When the Founders protested "taxation without representation," they were appealing to the Magna Carta.

Perhaps the most famous statement in the US Declaration of Independence is that "all men are created equal." Some philosophers and statesmen justified the concepts of universal human rights and equality without reference to the Bible. For many others, however, these principles were built upon biblical teachings on the dignity of human beings as bearers of the divine image.

Although the Magna Carta was not initially successful in accomplishing the peace for which it was intended, it was revised in later years and eventually set a standard, based on the Bible, that laid the foundation for the English system of common law. Today, our modern democratic society continues to reap the benefits. ■

Left: Magna Carta Libertatum.
Above: Tomb of King John of England. Buried in Worcester Cathedral.

14 Chartres Cathedral Is Consecrated

The Chartres Cathedral, located fifty miles from Paris, was consecrated in 1260. This architectural wonder has stood tall since the Middle Ages, and in 1979 it was named a UNESCO World Heritage Site (a place that is listed by the United Nations Educational, Scientific and Cultural Organization as having special cultural or physical significance).

This historic cathedral is considered to be one of the world's finest examples of Gothic architecture. Its unprecedented design pioneered several new architectural features and established revolutionary techniques for construction at high elevations. A structure that has largely remained intact since it was built, the

Chartres Cathedral showcases many elements of Gothic architecture, including pointed arches, rib-and-panel vaults, and flying buttresses. It also contains a labyrinth stone floor, a large astrological clock, and many stained-glass windows that depict biblical scenes. In its portals more than seven hundred statues and figures of biblical characters and church leaders stand beside narrative scenes that depict stories from the Bible.

This exquisite cathedral includes numerous biblical elements that reflect the Catholicism of the time and communicate the church's mission to teach and preach the gospel worldwide. ■

Above and Right: Cathedral Basilica of Our Lady of Chartres, France.

15 Thomas Aquinas Clarifies Christian Theology in Summa Theologica

Born in 1225 in a village in central Italy, Thomas Aquinas lived at a critical juncture of Western culture. When Thomas was young, his parents handed him over to a group of Benedictine monks. It was not unusual for wealthy Christian families at that time to secure a future for their youngest male offspring as a member of a religious order. Thomas later joined another religious order, the Dominicans, and began studying at the University of Paris.

At first, his fellow students misinterpreted Thomas's quiet nature as a sign of dullness. However, one professor, known later as Albert the Great, recognized his latent genius. "You call him the dumb ox," Albert said, "but in his teaching he will one day produce such a bellowing that it will be heard throughout the world."

Eventually Thomas became a teacher and professor. His magnum opus, a vast manual of Christian doctrine called *Summa Theologica*, proved Albert right.

Summa Theologica is an instructional guide designed to teach the Bible to beginning theological students and literate laypeople. It communicates in a clear and concise way the key points of Christian theology, including the existence of God, the creation of the world, the nature of man, virtues and vices, the person and work of Jesus, the sacraments, and the end of the world.

The *Summa* was intended as a systematic exposition of theology, a synthesis of faith and reason. Aquinas asserted that humans must employ their power of reasoning to gain knowledge of spiritual truth. Nature was God's handiwork, he argued, and therefore should be studied using the methods of logic and science. But Aquinas also held that reason alone was not sufficient. In his view, the deepest truths were found in the Bible, and they could be understood only through faith in what God revealed. Aquinas then used reason to defend and explain these truths. The writings of this thirteen-century Dominican philosopher became fundamental texts in Catholic theology. They also helped to open Christian academic thought to the scientific method.

Summa Theologica's impact on the church and the development of Christianity was extremely significant. One Catholic historian has said, "No single theological work in the history of Catholicism has had the impact of the *Summa*."[2]

While primarily a Christian work, the *Summa* also draws extensively from Hebrew, Muslim, and pagan sources. This is one reason it is considered one of the most influential works of Western literature. ∎

Above: Thomas Aquinas by Carlo Crivelli (ca. 1435–1495).

16

Petrarch Helps Launch the Renaissance

Born into a middle-class family in the fourteenth century, Francesco Petrarca (who later became known as Petrarch) was an Italian poet and scholar, most famous for having invented the sonnet. Petrarch is considered one of the greatest love poets of world literature, penning the 366 poems collected in his celebrated *Canzoniere*, or songbook.

As a young man, Petrarch demonstrated a love for the classics and displayed his deep Christian faith. He dedicated extensive time to studying the Bible, which he used as a daily guide in life. To Petrarch, the Bible was both true and a "source of nourishment . . . in the precepts for life it entails."[3] Because of this, the Bible was his most fundamental text. He was also influenced by the teachings of the early church fathers.

> *"Rarely do great beauty and great virtue dwell together."*
> – *Francesco Petrarca*

Petrarch took a position as a church cleric, which allowed him to travel around Europe, often searching for lost and forgotten texts. He felt it was his mission to save these classic works and preserve them for posterity. As he studied these ancient texts, Petrarch began to believe that humankind could once again achieve the kinds of accomplishments that were reflected in the Bible. This was the basis for the worldview he founded, which has come to be known as humanism. Petrarch believed that humankind, when modeled in God's image, could do amazing things. While humanism later became associated with secularism, Petrarch was a devout Christian and did not see a conflict between realizing humanity's potential and having religious faith.

Petrarch's writings and worldview inspired the humanist attitudes of fifteenth-century Italy that culminated in the Renaissance, a significant cultural movement that would not have been possible without him. ■

Right: Statue of Francesco Petrarca in Florence, Italy.

17 John Ball Emboldens the Peasants' Revolt

John Ball was an English traveling preacher who believed that all people were created equal (Galatians 2:6; Ephesians 6:9). As the Black Death swept through England, killing noblemen and peasants alike, the peasants began to question why they should be subject to the authority of the nobility.

A member of the Lollard movement, Ball believed that priests should embrace social equality and taught that anyone who was devout could celebrate Mass, whether they were lay or ordained. Convinced of the spiritual equality of all people, regardless of social class, Ball would meet people in the courtyard after church services and preach in English, the language of the people, rather than in Latin, the language of the clergy.

John was imprisoned because of his preaching about social equality and his methods, which were unpopular with the established church. His imprisonment triggered the Peasants' Revolt of 1381, an uprising whose goals were inspired by the principles he taught.

After the rebel peasants freed Ball from prison, they marched to London, where Ball addressed the group with an inspiring speech that repeated the people's demands for equality, based on the Bible's teachings about the garden of Eden. His famous quote questioning class distinctions has echoed down through the centuries: "When Adam delved and Eve span, who was then the gentleman?"[4] The following day the rebels, inspired by Ball's sermon, crossed London Bridge into the city.

The Peasants' Revolt was the first significant popular rebellion in English history. Historians credit this uprising as the beginning of the end for feudalism. ■

Above: Illustration of the priest John Ball on a horse encouraging Wat Tyler's rebels of 1381, from a ca. 1470 manuscript of Jean Froissart's *Chronicles* in the British Library.

18 Joan of Arc Leads France in Battle

A French peasant girl born in the 1300s, Jehanne le Pucelle (Joan the Maid) showed a tremendous amount of devotion to God. She was influenced greatly by the Bible, using it for a guidebook on how to live. She also attended confession daily and spent much of her time in church.

At the age of thirteen, Joan began hearing voices and experiencing visions. She understood these supernatural encounters to be instructing her to live piously and to lead the French soldiers against the English army. She joined the military when she was only seventeen years old, without any training. Determined that God would give her victory, Joan put on a suit of armor, rallied the French forces, and routed the English army in only nine days, becoming one of history's youngest military leaders. She accompanied the French soldiers with a banner that had a picture that represented God and the words *Jesus Maria* on it. She used this banner in place of a weapon.

During battle, Joan championed the humane treatment of captured soldiers. Unfortunately, this same standard was not given to her when she was caught, brought to trial, and then burned at the stake. Her death became the catalyst for French victory and elevated the view of women in society. ■

Above: *Entrance of Joan of Arc into Reims in 1429*, painting by Jan Matejko (1838–1893).
Right: Joan of Arc at the coronation of Charles VII in the cathedral of Reims, July 1429. Painted in 1854.

19 Johannes Gutenberg Prints the First Bible

For centuries scribes copied their manuscripts by hand, letter by letter, a meticulous and time-consuming process. But in fifteenth-century Europe, the growth of universities, the opening of new trade routes, and the increasingly common trade fairs created a growing demand for books. This demand meant that it was worth investing in a new way to produce books based on movable-type printing technology. While this technology had been in use in the Far East for centuries, the use of thousands of characters in Asian languages made Asian printing presses expensive and slow. Johannes Gutenberg developed a more mechanical version of the metal printing press in Europe and unleashed a printing revolution that changed the history of the West and ultimately the world.

Johannes Gutenberg was born in Mainz, Germany (ca. 1397). He worked as a blacksmith and goldsmith. In 1440, he unveiled a practical printing press that combined the use of a wooden printing press with oil-based ink and metallic components representing letters and punctuation marks that could be moved and reconfigured to print different pages. It also took advantage of high-quality parchment and paper made from rags.

The device worked like this: The movable-type pieces were arranged by hand and held together within a wooden form. Ink was rolled over the raised surfaces of the letters and punctuation marks on the type pieces. Then the form was pressed against a sheet of paper. In the time that it would take for a scribe to copy a handful of pages manually, Gutenberg's printing press could stamp out thousands of nearly identical pages. His remarkable invention made it possible to produce books on a massive scale without a massive cost.

One of the first books to be printed by Gutenberg was Western civilization's most influential literary creation. The Gutenberg Bible launched the age of printed books in the West.

This beautifully executed Bible used the text of the Latin translation known as the Vulgate, and Gutenberg spared no expense in producing his masterpiece. He used almost three hundred individual pieces of type, applied the finest inks, and determined the dimensions of each page with great precision.

The Gutenberg Bible heralded the new age of mass printing. It was an unrivaled creation, regarded by many as the finest book of all time. Sold at the 1455 Frankfurt Book Fair, the Gutenberg Bible became the first best seller in history, eagerly acquired by monasteries, universities, and (presumably) a small number of wealthy individuals.

Gutenberg once said, "God suffers in the multitude of souls whom His word cannot reach. Religious truth is imprisoned in a small number of manuscript books which confine instead of spread the public treasure. Let us break the seal which seals up holy things and give wings to Truth in order that she may win every soul."

Society has been greatly changed because of the impact of Gutenberg. His innovation led to a culture dominated by the printed word, which encouraged the power of individual thought. The printing press started an information revolution on par with that brought about by the Internet, by making the accumulated knowledge of the human race available to any person who could read. Very few innovations have had as great an impact on civilization as the Gutenberg Bible. ■

Left: The printing press invented by Johannes Gutenberg between 1397 and 1400.

20 Leonardo da Vinci Paints
The Last Supper

The most reproduced religious painting of all time is Leonardo da Vinci's *The Last Supper*. He began painting the mural in 1495 on a dining room wall in the monastery of Santa Maria delle Grazie in Milan, Italy. This painting was commissioned as part of the church's renovations, and da Vinci completed the work in 1498.

In the painting, da Vinci depicts the biblical scene of the last time Jesus ate with his disciples before his crucifixion (John 13:21–22). The faces of each disciple are shown the moment after they receive the news that one of them will betray Jesus.

Leonardo's creation is the best-known version of the event described in the New Testament, but other artists had their own views. Not long after Leonardo, the great Italian artist Jacopo Bassano painted a much livelier and more theatrical version in 1542. Many contemporary artists have recreated the work, including artists Salvador Dalí and Andy Warhol, and sculptor Marisol Escobar. Vik Muniz even made a version out of chocolate sauce. This is but one example of how a single biblical scene can be depicted in a nearly infinite number of ways.

Leonardo da Vinci's *The Last Supper* is one of the most famous paintings ever created, painted by one of the greatest artists of all time. It remains a popular, much-studied, and influential masterpiece. ■

Above: *The Last Supper* (1495–1498), Leonardo da Vinci (1452–1519), Santa Maria delle Grazie, Milan.

21 Michelangelo Carves the World's Greatest Statue

Born Michelangelo di Lodovico Buonarroti Simoni, Michelangelo was one of the greatest artistic masters of the Renaissance. Along with Leonardo da Vinci, he is remembered as a quintessential "Renaissance man."

Michelangelo's father owned a quarry. From a young age, the boy was chiseling away at stones. He was obsessed with his art. He was known to work and sleep in the same clothes for days at a time. And when he did get around to resting, he often slept with his boots on!

Michelangelo was only twenty-six years old when he was chosen to sculpt a colossal marble statue of David. In the Bible, David is the famed shepherd boy who defeated the giant Goliath with a sling and single stone (1 Samuel 17). Prior to this statue, earlier depictions of David typically showed him mid-swing or standing victorious over Goliath. Michelangelo shifted away from this pattern, apparently choosing instead to depict David before he killed Goliath, standing tense and combat-ready. He started carving a gigantic marble stone on September 13, 1501, and completed the sculpture in 1504.

This almost seventeen-foot-tall statue not only showcases Michelangelo's extraordinary technical skill but also became, for the city of Florence, a symbol of liberty and freedom.

The statue of David stands today in the Gallery of the Academy of Florence, an art museum in Florence, Italy. As one of the most recognized Renaissance sculptures of all time, this statue offers inspiration to many to stand tall against any opposition.

Centuries after his death, Michelangelo's body of work has yet to be surpassed. Michelangelo excelled in many areas, including sculpture, painting, architecture, poetry, and engineering. Because so many of his finished works, sketches, and personal papers have survived, Michelangelo is considered to be the best documented of all the Renaissance artists. ∎

Left: Michelangelo's statue of David.

Michelangelo was considered the greatest artist of his lifetime. He is well known for painting the Sistine Chapel, a feat that started as a commission given by Pope Julius II to Michelangelo to paint the twelve apostles on the ceiling of the Sistine Chapel and ended four years later as a masterpiece with more than 300 biblical figures, including nine different stories from Genesis.

No list of important Western art is complete without the Sistine Chapel. What is it about this work that has made this place so famous?

First, even half a millennium after its creation, the project's sheer scale remains awe-inspiring. The surface of the ceiling painted by Michelangelo covers about 5,400 square feet, a bit larger than an NBA basketball court. Over a four-year span, the great Renaissance artist single-handedly painted the entire surface in intricate detail.

Second, the conditions and requirements were extremely challenging. The ceiling was not only enormous; it was also sixty-five feet above the ground! Michelangelo stood on a wooden platform and craned his neck for many hours each day, so much so that he suffered severe headaches and spasms. (Michelangelo even wrote a poem about his misery.) To make matters worse, the plaster he was using turned moldy during the process, so he had to remove it and start anew. There were also problems with the original scaffolding built to support the artist; Michelangelo had to dismantle it and design and create a new platform.

Third, Michelangelo's finished ceiling was innovative in technical and artistic ways. Michelangelo brought a new sensibility to ceiling art that reflected his background as a sculptor and architect. He blended art and architecture in a pioneering manner that generations of subsequent artists have imitated. Prior to the Sistine Chapel, ornamentation was largely flat and two-dimensional. Michelangelo's experience with the chisel led him to merge decoration and architecture to produce breathtaking innovation. He achieved a sense of structure around the characters and scenes and infused the figures with a sense of power and weight, expression and movement, passion and intensity. Artists such as Raphael began emulating Michelangelo's techniques soon after viewing the ceiling.

Michelangelo's most recognizable fresco on the ceiling is his *Creation of Adam*, which illustrates the creation narrative from the Bible's book of Genesis. *The Creation of Adam* shows God reaching out to Adam, depicted in the fingers of Adam and God, which do not touch. Likewise, the scene shows God's right arm extended as if he is imparting life into Adam, whose left arm is extended in an echoing pose of God's. Through the depiction of God as the giver of life and Adam echoing God's pose, Michelangelo conveys the message that humanity is created in the image of God and is also dependent upon him.

The Creation of Adam fresco has been endlessly copied. From the poster promoting Steven Spielberg's movie *E.T. the Extra-Terrestrial* to a parody showing Jim Henson (creator of the Muppets) giving life to Kermit the Frog, Michelangelo's work continues to shape popular culture today.

Five centuries have passed since Michelangelo painted this iconic work inspired by the Bible, yet it still produces a sense of awe and appreciation for its unparalleled influence on the development of Western art.

23

Martin Luther Launches the Protestant Reformation

Martin Luther—a German theologian, priest, monk, composer, and Bible translator—is one of the most influential people in the history of Christianity.

In defiance of the practices of the church at the time, Luther rejected the claim that freedom from the punishment of sin could be purchased with money and other valuables. He used passages from the Bible such as Ephesians 2:8 ("For by grace you have been saved through faith. And this is not your own doing; it is the gift of God") to teach that salvation is accomplished with God's grace only through faith in Jesus. He also challenged the authority of the pope by teaching that the Bible is the only source of divine knowledge.

On October 31, 1517, Luther famously nailed his Ninety-Five Theses to the door of Wittenberg's Castle Church. This list of Luther's opinions and questions about accepted church practices launched the Protestant Reformation.

Luther's translation of the Bible from the Latin into German impacted both the church and German culture. For the first time, German laypeople could read the Bible themselves, and Luther's widely read translation contributed to the development of a standard German language. His work also influenced the Tyndale Bible, the first mass-produced English translation.

Luther's refusal to renounce his teachings and his writings resulted in his excommunication by Pope Leo X and his condemnation by the Holy Roman Emperor Charles V at the Diet of Worms. However, his ideas shaped Protestantism and eventually helped change the course of history. ∎

"Peace if possible, truth at all costs."
– Martin Luther

Top: *Martin Luther* (1529) by Lucas Cranach (1472–1553).

Right: All Saints' Church in Wittenberg, Germany, where Martin Luther nailed the Ninety-Five Theses on the door and sparked the Reformation.

24 Ferdinand Magellan Sails to Spread Christianity

As leader of the first voyage to circumnavigate the globe, Portuguese explorer Ferdinand Magellan cultivated a legacy that goes beyond merely making his mark in history as an explorer.

Magellan set out from Spain in 1519 with a fleet of five ships to discover a western sea route to the Spice Islands. Along the way he discovered what is now known as the Strait of Magellan and became the first European to cross the Pacific Ocean. Magellan's legendary voyage around the world claimed the lives of many people and forever changed how people in Europe understood world geography.

Magellan's expedition also had a far-reaching impact beyond the geographical sphere. Magellan was a zealous evangelist who sought to convert the native people he encountered to Christianity. One notable example was the conversion of Chief Humabon of Cebu (Philippines), whom Magellan baptized along with thousands of his subjects. Ultimately, Magellan's religious fervor cost him his life. Chief Humabon asked Magellan to travel to the island of Mactan to kill his enemy, Chief Lapu-Lapu. Magellan saw this as an opportunity to convert more people to Christianity. He arrived with good intentions, only to be greeted by a battle that resulted in his death.

Despite his ill-fated death, Magellan's legacy lives on—both for his significant contributions to world geography and his contribution to church history. If Magellan had stifled his religious fervor, the teachings of the Bible may not have been introduced to the many lands he traveled to until much later. ∎

Above: Illustration of Ferdinand Magellan passing his strait, 1890.

25

William Tyndale's English Translation Impacts Society

Prior to the Vulgate—the Latin version of the Bible translated by Jerome between 382 and 420—the only Latin translations of the Bible that existed were known as *Vetus Latina*. By the sixteenth century, the Vulgate became the only authorized translation of the Bible. Only the wealthy and educated in England were able to read Latin, so they held power within the Church of England.

William Tyndale, an English scholar and theologian, set out to translate the Bible into the common language. He did this at great risk, enduring threats of imprisonment. Traveling to London to seek permission to translate the Bible into English, Tyndale found himself at a dead end after being denied assistance from Bishop Cuthbert Tunstall. He set out from London for Germany, where there were numerous Protestants who were much more favorable to Tyndale's task at hand.

The Bible's availability in the language of the commoner had a significant impact. It played a role in the restructuring of power in England, since the common person could now understand the Bible and pursue faith without the influence of the elitist power structure. Tyndale eventually paid the price for bringing an English-language Bible to the commoners. He was burned at the stake for inciting what the authorities viewed as unrest and rebellion. ∎

Right: A Tyndale Bible, displayed at the Bodleian Library. Photo courtesy of Steve Bennett.

26 Nicolaus Copernicus Reveals an Orderly Creator

Born in Poland in the sixteenth century, Nicolaus Copernicus showed religious faith at a young age by working in a cathedral and serving as a physician to the poor. The Bible was his foundation for all his scientific views. He said, "The universe has been wrought for us by a supremely good and orderly Creator."

Copernicus sought to seek the truth in all things, convinced that God granted people the ability to discern truth through human reason. His text *On the Revolutions* was an effort to express this view to the pope. In this document, he refuted the long-held view that the earth was the center of the universe and proposed an alternate view that the planets instead revolve around the sun—a fact that did not in any way diminish God's great care in creation, as revealed in the Bible.

Because the idea of a sun-centered universe contradicted the church's teachings at the time, Copernicus was viewed as antireligious. However, Copernicus appealed to Pope Paul II in his dedication, writing, "I can easily conceive, most Holy Father, that as soon as some people learn that in this book which I have written concerning the revolutions of the heavenly bodies, I ascribe certain motions to the Earth, they will cry out at once that I and my theory should be rejected." Copernicus, a devoutly religious man, was not attempting to go against the church. Rather, he simply purposed to tell the truth that he had discovered through his scientific observations.

> *"Of all things visible, the highest is the heaven of the fixed stars."*
>
> – *Nicolaus Copernicus*

Widely hailed as the founder of modern astronomy, Copernicus, with his model of a sun-centered planetary system, provided a strong foundation for future scientists to build on in order to improve our understanding of the motion of heavenly bodies. ▪

27 Tycho Brahe Revolutionizes Astronomy

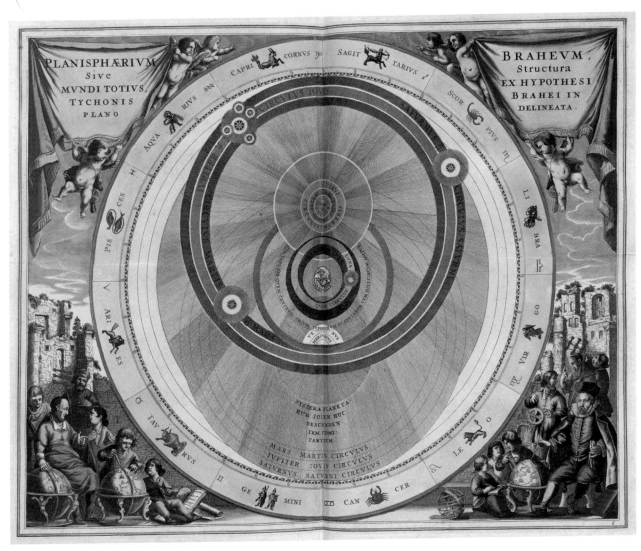

Tycho Brahe was an astronomer, astrologer, and alchemist whose contributions to astronomy far surpassed those of his contemporaries. He also sought to better understand the mind of God as he studied the mysteries of the universe.

Brahe designed and constructed various astronomical instruments, and he also calibrated them and checked them for accuracy. In doing so, he revolutionized astronomical instrumentation, profoundly changing how the universe is observed. Unlike other astronomers who merely observed the positions of planets and the moon at certain important points of their orbits, Brahe observed these bodies throughout their orbits. His observations were five times more accurate than the best available observations at the time. They documented numerous orbital anomalies that had never been noticed before.

Brahe's revolutionary work not only provided a deeper appreciation for the intricacies of the universe but also validated that scientific knowledge is evidenced in the Bible. Brahe's vast contributions confirm the complexity and beauty of the universe of which the Bible attests. ■

Above: The planisphere of Brahe, or the structure of the universe following the hypothesis of Tycho Brahe drawn in a planar view.

28 Francis Bacon Develops the Scientific Method

Sir Francis Bacon was born into a life of privilege, only to have it stripped away upon his father's death in 1579. Having been ruined politically and financially, he began writing.

Bacon was a student of the Bible, which greatly influenced his work and his writing. His biblical knowledge was especially beneficial in his work on editing the King James Bible in 1611. After his death, he left many annotations in his copy of the Bible and scores of work in theology. Mixing his scientific theories with his religious beliefs, Bacon believed that "knowledge is the rich storehouse for the glory of the Creator and the relief of man's estate."

Bacon is best known for discovering and popularizing the scientific method. In his new method, scientific laws are able to be discovered by analyzing data gathered from a series of experiments and observations, rather than from logic-based arguments. Scientists then test possible truths, or hypotheses, by using this method to set up experiments to attempt to prove their hypotheses wrong.

> *"Knowledge is the rich storehouse for the glory of the Creator and the relief of man's estate."*
> – *Sir Francis Bacon*

Bacon's scientific method marked the beginning of the end for the 2,000-year-old natural philosophy of Aristotle, unleashing a wave of new scientific discoveries. Without Bacon's contributions, modern scientific inquiry may not have been possible. ■

Left: *Sir Francis Bacon* (ca. 1618).

29 Johannes Kepler Originates Intelligent Design

Johannes Kepler was a central figure in the Scientific Revolution. A German mathematician, astronomer, and astrologer, Kepler is best known for his laws of planetary motion.

Many of the scientists who were part of the Scientific Revolution believed that science could demonstrate the wonders of creation and its creator. Kepler discussed his work as a "sacred discourse." Guided by his conviction of the inspiration and authority of the Bible, Kepler incorporated religious arguments and reasoning into his work. He sought to find a connection between the physical and spiritual world. Because the universe was designed by an intelligent creator, Kepler reasoned, then it should function according to a logical pattern.

Kepler's work focused on his conviction that God created the world according to an intelligible plan. From his thorough analysis of astronomical data, he realized that planets move in elliptical—not circular—orbits. This included how the planets traveled around the sun. Kepler incorporated this understanding in his famed laws of planetary motion.

Today, Kepler's observations help us understand how the positions of the planets, sun, moon, and stars affect the seasons of the year and the tides. This knowledge is applied in our modern world in the many industries that are affected by the phases of the moon, such as fishing, agriculture, and even military planning. ■

Above: Portrait of Johannes Kepler. Copy of a lost original from 1610 in the Benedictine monastery in Kremsmünster.

30 Miguel de Cervantes Writes the First Modern Novel

Considered the first modern novel and regarded among the best works of fiction ever written, Miguel de Cervantes's *Don Quixote* is filled with biblical ideals and explores the complex and contradictory themes of fact and fantasy, truth and lies, justice and injustice.

Cervantes's novel follows the adventures of a Spanish gentleman named Alonso Quixano who sets out to revive chivalry, undo wrongs, and bring justice to the world under the name Don Quixote de la Mancha. Don Quixote recruits a simple peasant, Sancho Panza, as his squire. Sancho assists Don Quixote in his attempt to revive chivalry and establish a more compatible system of morality.

Cervantes contrasts the peasant Sancho's compassion and thoughtfulness with the duke and duchess's thoughtless malice. In this way he challenges the conventional belief that aristocrats are automatically respectable and noble. This theme reflects the biblical principle that no preference is to be given or any favoritism shown to the rich while the poor are treated with less worth (James 2:1–7). Cervantes's distinction between a person's class and a person's worth was a radical idea in his era, serving as a primary reason that *Don Quixote* was such a revolutionary work in its time. ∎

**Top: Portrait of Miguel de Cervantes.
Above: Windmills of Consuegra Castle, La Mancha region of Spain. Consuegra's windmills became famous in the 16th century, when *Don Quixote* was first published.**

31 John Rolfe Promotes Christianity in the New World

In the early years of the seventeenth century, England established colonies in America with hopes of reaping great economic gain. However, not every colonist had wealth as the top motivation for leaving England. Aside from colonial expansion, Jamestown—the first English settlement in North America—was established for economic and religious reasons.

The pursuits of the English in the New World did not bode well for the native inhabitants. In contrast, John Rolfe, a devout Christian settler, pursued the possibility that biblical teachings could be useful to the natives. He pointed out that the image of God, as revealed in the Genesis account of creation, could be witnessed in the natives also. Rolfe married Pocahontas, the daughter of a native chief, after her conversion to Christianity. Because of their marriage, peace existed for a time between the colonists and the native inhabitants.

While many early settlers of America treated their new land and its people with mixed motives of greed and pride, there were those, like Rolfe, who desired to bring the teachings of the Bible to the people in the New World. ■

Above: Remains of the 1639 Jamestown Church tower (with 20th-century reconstruction on the original foundations).

32 Galileo Seeks to Harmonize Religion and Science

Galileo is often called the father of observational astronomy. The first astronomer to use a telescope to study the heavens, Galileo revolutionized the science of astronomy. His findings had a major impact on the Scientific Revolution.

Galileo's discovery that Jupiter had four moons challenged long-held views about the universe. He also discovered imperfections in the sun, a huge number of stars in the Milky Way, and the changing phases of Venus. Most importantly, Galileo's observations revealed flaws in the church's long-held view of celestial objects. Galileo proposed that, contrary to Aristotle's view of an earth-centered solar system, ours is a sun-centered solar system. Because of this, Galileo's work was potentially heretical to the church.

At the time of Galileo, the church—and most educated persons—believed the earth was the center of the universe. They believed the geocentric model was consistent with biblical texts that describe how the earth cannot be moved (1 Chronicles 16:30; Psalms 93:1, 104:5) or how the sun rises and sets and returns to its place (Ecclesiastes 1:5). It was considered well supported by the Bible and the stars that the earth was the center of the universe.

Galileo promoted heliocentrism much more strongly than Copernicus had done about a century earlier. Then, in his letter in 1615 to the Grand Duchess Christina, Galileo appealed to one of the great Christian theologians, Augustine, to argue that poetic passages in the Bible were not meant to be interpreted literally. This letter aroused a good deal of anger. It was taken to be arrogant and insulting toward many who were open to scientific argumentation.

In 1616, the church declared heliocentrism was contrary to good science and good theology. Galileo was forbidden to teach that heliocentrism was true, and books promoting heliocentrism were banned. In 1633, Galileo was convicted of heresy and condemned to house arrest for the rest of his life.

In response, Galileo explained the Bible was not intended to teach astronomy but rather to "persuade men of the truths necessary for salvation." In a letter to Duchess Christina, Galileo argued that the Bible teaches

"I give infinite thanks to God, who has been pleased to make me the first observer of marvelous things." –Galileo

"how to go to heaven, not how the heavens go." Galileo had a high view of God and of the Bible. He said, "I give infinite thanks to God, who has been pleased to make me the first observer of marvelous things."[5] Galileo once wrote in a letter, "The Holy Scriptures cannot err and the decrees therein contained are absolutely true and inviolable. I should have added that, though scripture cannot err, its expounders and interpreters are liable to err in many ways."

Galileo's scientific discoveries present us with a view of the universe as beautifully constructed by God. Convinced of the strong relationship between religion and science, Galileo attested, "God is known by nature in his works, and by doctrine in his revealed word."[6] ■

The planet Jupiter with one of its orbiting moons, Europa.

33 The King James Bible Is Published

In 1604 King James convened the Hampton Court Conference, which proposed to create a new English version of the Bible that could be widely printed and distributed. The King James Version, as it has come to be known, was created by a team of elite scholars and first published in 1611. Hailed as a work of literary genius, this King James Version is still considered by many to be the most authoritative version of the Bible in the English language.

With its significant impact on the English language, it would be impossible to imagine English without the everyday phrases the Bible has added to it.

One popular expression that is rooted in the Bible is the phrase "by the skin of my teeth" (Job 19:20). Furthermore, ask yourself: Who hasn't suffered a "broken heart" (Psalm 34:18)? The expression "go the extra mile" is derived from Matthew 5:41. In Luke 10:25–37, we hear of the "good Samaritan," which reminds us of the principle of doing good deeds. The phrase "getting to the root of the matter" (Job 19:28) reminds us that we need to seek the source of where something begins so we can determine the truth.

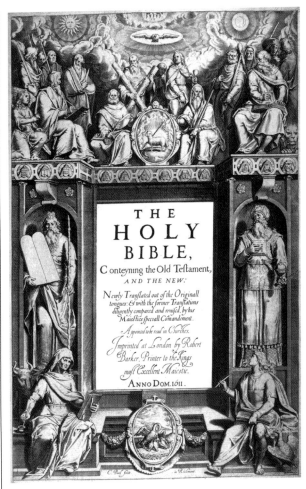

Traces of biblical influence live on in the language we speak every day. Other examples of familiar phrases that derive from the King James Bible include the following: "Be fruitful, and multiply" (Genesis 1:22), "God forbid" (Genesis 44:7), "There is no new thing under the sun" (Ecclesiastes 1:9), "Two are better than one" (Ecclesiastes 4:9), "Woe is me!" (Isaiah 6:5), "an eye for an eye" (Matthew 5:38), "The last shall be first" (Matthew 19:30), "den of thieves" (Matthew 21:13), "It is more blessed to give than to receive" (Acts 20:35), "in the twinkling of an eye" (1 Corinthians 15:52), and "a thief in the night" (1 Thessalonians 5:2).

Over time, the King James Bible irrevocably shaped the English language, creating a language framework used in arts, politics, and everyday conversation. ∎

Right: The title page to the 1611 first edition of the Authorized Version of the Bible.
Above: Portrait of King James by Daniel Mytens.

34 The Pilgrims Seek Religious Freedom in the New World

During the seventeenth century, the Church of England was the same as the government of England. Because of this, King James was head of both the country and the church. Consequently, not belonging to the church meant not obeying the king, an act that was considered to be treason.

A group of English people known as Pilgrims wanted a safe place to practice their religion. In September 1620 they left England for America on the merchant ship called the *Mayflower*. Ships of that time typically hauled cargo for trade, but on this particular trip the *Mayflower* carried 102 passengers, mostly Pilgrims.

When the *Mayflower* arrived on the shores of Cape Cod, in present-day Massachusetts, the Pilgrims had hopes of making a better life for themselves and their children, while also being able to worship freely. The Mayflower Compact explains that their journey across the ocean was "undertaken, for the Glory of God and advancement of the Christian Faith."[7] They covenanted to work together in a "Civil Body Politic, for [their] better ordering and preservation."[8] The Pilgrims' perseverance laid the foundation for a new world that would be grounded in religious freedom.

Given the Pilgrims' expressed motives to establish Massachusetts, it should be no surprise that this colony's early laws were filled with references to the Bible, biblical concepts, and biblical language. The Laws and Liberties of Massachusetts is one of the most clearly biblical of the early legal codes in America, citing Bible verses throughout.

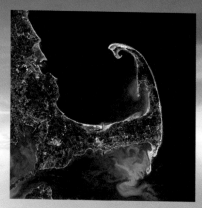

Cape Cod is an arm-shaped peninsula forming the easternmost portion of the Commonwealth of Massachusetts where the *Mayflower* first landed.

"Having undertaken, for the Glory of God and advancement of the Christian Faith."
– *The Mayflower Compact*

Mayflower II replica at sunset, Massachusetts.

35 Massachusetts Founds Harvard University to Train Clergy

Some 17,000 Puritans—loyal members of the Church of England who sought to reform the church—migrated from England to America by 1636. Their leaving was in large part due to the efforts of the Pilgrims, who had settled in New England after completely breaking from the Church of England rather than attempting to reform it.

The Puritans wanted to ensure that New England's growing population would be served by local pastors who were educated in the Bible and equipped to serve their newly established churches. So on September 8, 1636, the Puritans founded the first formal institution of higher learning in the American colonies. Originally called the New College, it was renamed Harvard College in 1639 after its first benefactor, Reverend John Harvard, passed away, bequeathing his library and half of his estate to the new institution. The early motto of Harvard was *Veritas Christo et Ecclesiae*—"Truth for Christ and the Church" (now simply *Veritas*).

The determined efforts by the Puritans to educate and train clergy created opportunities for biblical academic pursuit in the New World. Harvard's founders established the school for a specific purpose. They stated, "One of the next things we longed for and looked after was to advance learning and perpetuate it to posterity; dreading to leave an illiterate ministry to the churches, when our present ministers shall lie in the dust."[9] ∎

Above: Massachusetts Hall, Harvard University. Built in 1720, it is Harvard's oldest building.

36 René Descartes Sets Foundation for Modern Philosophy

René Descartes—the man who would become known as the father of modern philosophy—started his education at a Jesuit college at age eight. He dedicated his life to the extensive pursuit of true knowledge using the Bible as his primary source.

Always thinking, Descartes strove to apply mathematics and logic to the natural world around him. This was the basis for his mind-body duality and his famous quote, "I think, therefore I am."

Descartes's deeply rooted faith drove him to create his philosophical foundations and inspired him to try to reason the existence of God. Descartes justified his search for natural laws on the ground that God is perfect, and therefore perfect and unchanging laws must exist.

"I think, therefore I am."
– René Descartes

Descartes is often regarded as the first major figure in the philosophical movement known as rationalism, a way of understanding the world based on the use of reason. Descartes felt that God wants humans to trust their senses and use logic to seek and discover the truth.

He wanted his philosophy of rationalism to be adopted by the Catholic Church as standard teaching. This never happened. Instead, Descartes's work became a foundation for the study of modern philosophy. In fact, much of contemporary Western philosophy is based on Descartes's writings, which students of philosophy still study today. ■

37 Blaise Pascal Integrates Reason and Faith

Blaise Pascal was a French mathematician and physicist who has been called one of the greatest and most influential mathematical writers of all time. He laid the foundation for modern probability theory and was an expert in many fields, as well as an influential religious philosopher.

As a mathematician, Blaise Pascal insisted on the need for both reason and faith. This was how he believed people would be able to find order in the world and understand the Bible.

Pascal's research led to the invention of the syringe, the hydraulic press, and an early form of the digital calculator. His studies relied heavily on his biblical view of an ordered world. Pascal believed that the physical world is capable of being studied, measured, and explored. However, he did not solely rely upon reason to understand the world around him. For all that is knowable, there are many situations that reason alone cannot explain. This, according to Pascal, is where faith comes in. This understanding of faith and reason set him apart from other Enlightenment-era thinkers.

People often assume that the Bible and faith are set in opposition to reason. Yet Pascal's persistent pursuit of faith, based on the Bible, helped him see beyond what is measurable. ∎

> *"There are two kinds of people one can call reasonable: those who serve God with all their heart because they know him, and those who seek him with all their heart because they do not know him."*
>
> *– Blaise Pascal*

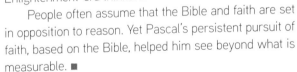

Above: Calculating machine designed by French mathematician Blaise Pascal in 1642 when he was nineteen years old.

38

Rembrandt Finds Inspiration in Biblical Stories

Like his contemporaries in the art world of the seventeenth century, Rembrandt Harmenszoon van Rijn, known simply as Rembrandt, created portraits, self-portraits, still lifes, and landscapes. However, he is perhaps best known for his paintings of scenes from the Bible.

Rembrandt depicted dozens of biblical themes. He often used ordinary people in his native city of Amsterdam as models, including many local Jews. He thought they would give him a more accurate sense of what people may have looked like in biblical times. Rembrandt is famous for his attempts at melding the earthly with the heavenly, and for his skillful use of light and shadows. Around seventy-five of his original masterpieces survive today.

As a significant member of the Dutch Golden Age of painting, Rembrandt's subject matter reflected the opulent and lavish style of his times. However, his biblical paintings, drawings, and etchings were atypical in that they often revealed the relationships of the people in the Bible with each other. In works such as *Christ and the Samaritan at the Well* (1659), *Peter Denies Christ* (1660), and *Supper at Emmaus* (1648), the Dutch master offered uniquely intimate glimpses of the people experiencing those events.

Art experts have called Rembrandt one of art's greatest storytellers. He used light and shade to present a realism that did not shy away from what might be considered unattractive. This set him apart from other baroque artists.

Since his paintings hang in the world's best museums today, Rembrandt continues to share his love of the Bible with the world. ■

Left: *The Return of the Prodigal Son* (ca. 1668–1669) by Rembrandt (1606–1669).

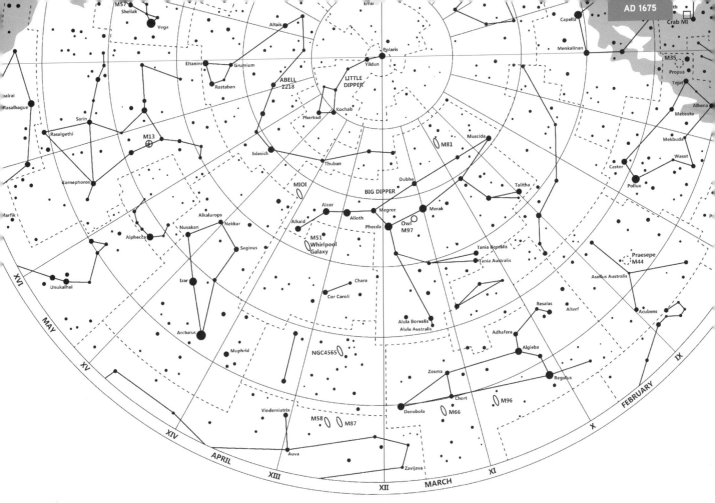

(39) John Flamsteed Opposes Agnostic Astronomers

John Flamsteed was the court astronomer to King Charles II of England, the first Astronomer Royal, and a contemporary of Sir Isaac Newton and Edmund Halley. Flamsteed felt that Halley was a bad influence on Newton. Because of this he would often send Newton biblical passages, such as Jeremiah 10:1–10, to warn him against associating with agnostic false prophets like Halley.

Flamsteed is not as well known as Newton and Halley, but his contributions in the field of astronomy are very impressive. He is famous for cataloging the stars in his *Historia Coelestis Britannica* (British Catalog of the Heavens), which was published in 1712. Additionally, his atlas of the stars, *Atlas Coelestis*, and his observation that comets returned along elliptical orbits are well known.

Flamsteed was devout in his Christian faith, showing a fascination with the Bible's story of creation and its confirmation of an order to the universe. Because of this, he struggled to see how any true astronomer could not believe in God. ∎

Above: Bust of John Flamsteed in the Museum of the Royal Greenwich Observatory, London.

40 Gottfried Leibniz Discovers Calculus

Gottfried Wilhelm Leibniz, a German mathematician and philosopher, is best known as one of the creators of calculus. Leibniz, a Lutheran who was born more than a century after Martin Luther, was also a well-known rationalist philosopher and amateur theologian. His interest in both religious knowledge and secular knowledge was reflected in his ability to see both sides of an argument. In books like *The Monadology* and *Theodicy*, Leibniz expands at length on his vision of the universe as being in line with the biblical cosmos.

Leibniz's books focus on the creation account in the first two chapters of the Bible's book of Genesis. Chapters 2 and 3 of *Theodicy* expand on his fascination with the Bible's teachings on the creation, fall, and redemption of humans. ■

Above: *The Expulsion of Adam and Eve from Paradise* (1791) by Benjamin West (1738–1820).

41 Robert Boyle Endeavors to Spread Christianity

Robert Boyle—known as the father of modern chemistry—has been hailed as the most important scientist ever born in Ireland.

Boyle was not only a chemist but also a philosopher, inventor, and devout Christian. He was the first person to establish chemistry as a separate science, and he was the first scientist to perform controlled experiments and then publish the details of his experiments—including particulars about the procedure, apparatus, and observations. His experiments with vacuums produced Boyle's law: The volume of a gas varies inversely with its pressure.

While serving as director of the East India Company, Boyle gave generously to missionary societies and funded Bible translation. He strongly believed the Bible should be available in the common language of the people. To ensure this, Boyle spared no expense in funding translations of the Bible in Welsh, Irish, and non-Western languages so people could have access to it in their native language.

The influence of the East India Company in numerous Eastern locales served as a great asset for Boyle's efforts to spread Christianity. The company expanded trading operations into Portugal and India, also establishing trading posts in Madras, Bombay, and Calcutta. Unfortunately, the company experienced a tragic piracy incident in 1695, resulting in the plunder of one of its most treasure-laden ships. This resulted in serious consequences for the business, including the closure of four of their factories in India and the imprisonment of their officers.

Boyle made the East India Company a dominant business in Asia. Even after the tragic piracy event, he remained influential and continued to spread Christianity in Eastern Asia.

In his last will and testament, Boyle wished the members of the Royal Society of London success "in their laudable attempts to discover the true Nature of the Works of God." In the minds of these scientists, scientific knowledge complemented the Bible and enriched their knowledge of God. ■

Above: *The Trading Post of the Dutch East India Company in Hooghly, Bengal* (1665) by Hendrik van Schuylenburgh (ca. 1620–1689), Dutch colonial painting, oil on panel. On the left is the Ganges River.

42

William Penn Founds Pennsylvania as a "Holy Experiment"

During a time of turmoil among Native Americans and colonists in the New World, William Penn's Quaker ideals drove his "Holy Experiment" of founding a Pennsylvania colony, a place based on a vision of true religious freedom. This meant the colony needed no military to fight off Native Americans, and the colonists there believed the Native Americans should be treated fairly.

These ideals were in sharp contrast to those of the other colonies, which warred with Native Americans over land. This attitude was unique because the land had been given to Penn for the colony charter by King Charles II. Still, Penn believed that taking the land from the people without paying them fairly was unjust.

> *"Men must be governed by God or they will be ruled by tyrants."*
>
> – William Penn

Despite other colonies claiming biblical principles in rejecting Native Americans based on their lack of civility and Christianity, Penn's Quaker interpretation of the Bible would not allow for this. He believed the Native Americans were also God's children and should be treated as such. Penn believed that God would bless his colony for its efforts to find peace and understanding with the Native Americans. His "Holy Experiment" provided a unique place for positive relations between the Native Americans and the colonists. ■

Top: *Admiral Sir William Penn*, Peter Lely (1618–1680).
Below: *The Treaty of Penn with the Indians*, 1771.

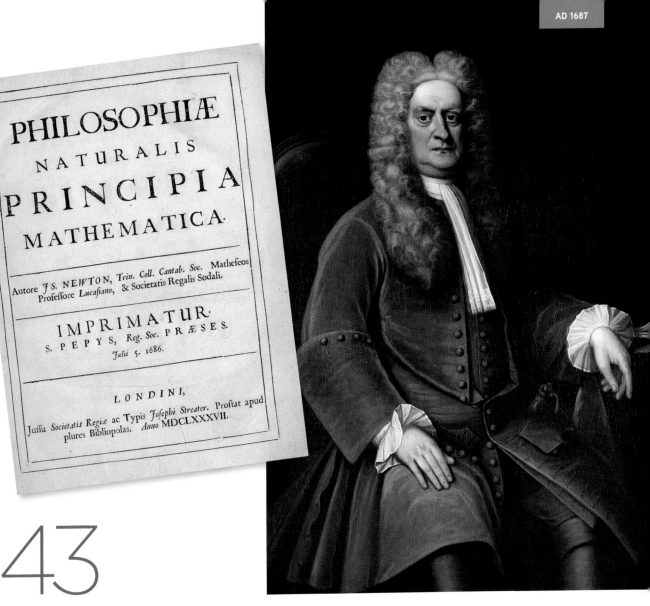

43

Isaac Newton Makes Scientific Breakthroughs

Sir Isaac Newton, one of the most well-known names in science, has been called the most influential scientist of the seventeenth century. Isaac Newton's *Philosophiæ Naturalis Principia* revealed scientific breakthroughs that formed the basis for modern physics and forever changed the way the world saw science. The *Principia* is considered by many to be among the most important works of scientific literature ever published.

Newton's biblical knowledge was the foundation for his landmark discoveries. His *Principia* introduced the laws of motion and set forth the ideas of classical mechanics. This book also explains Newton's universal law of gravitation, a concept studied by students of science around the world.

Experts today say that the true genius of Newton's work lies in how he took those theories and applied them to the universe at large, explaining the motions of the sun and planets in a way that had never been done before.

The scientific marvels that Newton set forth in his *Principia* are inspired from his biblical understanding of God as the creator of all things. The way Newton saw it, scientific inquiry could not function without a creator. He applied the Bible's teaching that God is in all things and works through all things to his scientific studies. Newton declared, "This most beautiful system of the sun, planets, and comets, could only proceed from the counsel and dominion of an intelligent and powerful Being."[10] ■

Above: Portrait of Sir Isaac Newton, oil on canvas.

44 John Locke Creates the Social Contract Theory

John Locke, the famous English philosopher, is considered the father of classical liberalism. His work *A Letter Concerning Toleration* outlines his views on religious tolerance. He was influenced by various Baptist theologians and by the Presbyterian poet John Milton.

John Locke's concept of humanity's God-given freedom helped prepare the American colonies to break away from England. His social contract theory stated that the people's natural right of freedom in a society allows for revolution when the government oversteps its boundaries. This theory provided traction for the newly formed United States to move toward freedom and independence.

John Locke read the Bible within the framework of natural freedom. According to the various passages in the Bible, certain rights and liberties are inherent in humanity's natural state. God's love for the whole world, expressed in John 3:16, is equally spread across humanity. He argued that God has given all people certain rights—such as the right to life, liberty, and property—that have a foundation independent from the laws of any specific government.

Locke believed this God-given freedom of the people may be partially lent to the government for the betterment of society. Since the government was only a government by the agreement of the people, the government could not restrict this freedom. ■

John Locke. Engraved by James Posselwhite (1798–1884) and published in *The Gallery of Portraits: With Memoirs,* vol. 5, by Thomas Malkin (London, 1835).

45 The English Bill of Rights Guarantees Freedom

The English Bill of Rights was the first document in world history to ensure humanity's natural rights. It also put a check on unrestrained power of the monarchy. This bloodless revolution, as it were, ensured that no English monarch had the power to do as they pleased—including imposing a national religion.

The Bible, and the perceived natural rights drawn from its teachings, was foundational to the development and establishment of the English Bill of Rights. This is relayed through two key topics in the document—equality and toleration, both of which were discussed by John Locke, the English philosopher who used biblical concepts to help ground his theories of natural law. Genesis 1:26, Matthew 13, and Luke 9 are biblical passages that influenced the writers of this great document in powerful ways. As a result of their Bill of Rights, the English people were given freedoms never before seen in history. This included the freedom to speak, to challenge monarchs, and most importantly, to worship. ■

Above Left and Right:
The English Bill of Rights established King William III of Orange and Queen Mary II of Britain as the nation's monarchs.
Right: Statue of William III of Orange, king from 1689 to 1702.

46 American Classrooms Use the Bible as a Primary Text

Early American school curriculum was greatly influenced by the Bible's texts and teachings. Educators such as Frederick A. Packard wrote, "No child should leave a daily public school in our country ignorant of the generally received principles of the Christian faith." Horace Mann said that "our system earnestly inculcates all Christian morals" and "welcomes the religion of the Bible." Mann once reported that the Bible was used "in almost all the schools, either as a devotional or as a reading book."

Prior to public schools, church was the elementary education for many children. After public school became more commonplace, it was seen as a supplement to learning that took place in the home or at church. The use of the Bible as a text in the classroom was a natural progression for many teachers.

The desire to read the Bible inspired many people to want to learn to read and to teach their children to read as well. It also shaped the way in which reading was taught in America. The *New England Primer*—the most successful educational textbook published in early America—is an excellent example.

The earliest English settlers in America used schoolbooks they had brought from England. In the

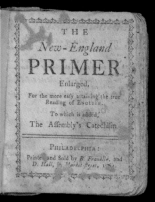

1680s, however, publishers in Boston began to issue a textbook adapted for the colonies called the *New England Primer*. Continually reissued in many editions in the 1700s, the primer taught the basics of a classical education as well as Christian character and Bible reading. Various versions of the primer included Bible passages from the King James Version, the "Lord's Prayer" (Matthew 6:9–13), and summaries of basic Christian belief called catechisms. Bible stories were presented in simple rhymes.

The *New England Primer* gives us a glimpse inside early colonial schoolhouses and shows us how deeply the Bible was embedded in American education. Scholars estimate that two to three million copies of the primer were sold over the course of 150 years. Although it was eventually replaced, the *New England Primer* shaped the way many generations of Americans learned to read and think. ∎

"No child should leave a daily public school in our country ignorant of the generally received principles of the Christian faith."
– Frederick A. Packard

47 Johann Sebastian Bach Composes Beloved Worship Music

Few composers in history have influenced music more than Johann Sebastian Bach. Born in Germany during the seventeenth century, Bach showed genius at an early age. By age fifteen he had already conducted choirs and written musical compositions. Eventually, Bach took a position as music and choir director of Saint Thomas Church in Germany, where he composed at a rate of one cantata per week!

Bach's *St. Matthew Passion* is considered a musical masterpiece and one of the highest cultural achievements of Western civilization, as his music and dedication to God are intertwined. The Bible was an integral source of inspiration for Bach. His music was his way of expressing his faith.

Bach made notes in the margins of his Bible. Adjacent to 1 Chronicles 25 he wrote, "This chapter is the true foundation of all God-pleasing music." And near 2 Chronicles 5:13 are the following words: "At a reverent performance of music, God is always at hand with his gracious presence."[11] ■

Above left: St. Thomas Church in Leipzig, Germany, where Johann Sebastian Bach worked as music director and where he was buried.

48

George Frideric Handel's *Messiah* Celebrates the Life of Jesus

Born in Germany in 1685, Baroque composer George Frideric Handel later became a naturalized English citizen. When Handel wasn't writing Italian operas, he was writing church music. Most of his works were written for the organ and contain biblical themes. *Dixit Dominus* (1707), for example, uses the Latin text of Psalms 110 and 126.

Perhaps one of the most famous pieces of music ever written or performed is Handel's masterpiece, *Messiah*. An interesting fact about *Messiah* is that, although it is now usually performed at Christmastime, it was originally an Easter piece. To create it, Handel took various Bible passages that had been carefully compiled by a friend named Charles Jennens and put the words to music. Jennens chose to include the story of Jesus as told in the Gospels and portions of the Hebrew Bible that he believed to be prophecies about the Messiah. For example, *Messiah* contains lyrics about the angel appearing to the shepherds in Luke 2:8–20 and "Comfort ye, comfort ye my people" from Isaiah 40:1 (KJV). Eventually, this highly acclaimed oratorio became associated with Christmas, largely due to the composition's "Hallelujah" chorus, which sets the announcement of Jesus's birth to choir, strings, and brass.

At the time, Handel's exciting musical accounts of the story of Jesus were considered blasphemous. Today, a broad and diverse audience appreciates his work for its inspiration. ■

George Frideric Handel, from *Meyers Lexicon* books.

49 Antoine Lavoisier Helps Invent Modern Chemistry

Antoine Lavoisier is best known for his studies that paved the way for modern chemistry. As a devout Catholic, Lavoisier did not see any contradiction between his scientific studies and his faith. He once complimented the English writer Edward King for "upholding revelation and the authenticity of the Holy Scripture."[12]

Lavoisier lived during a time when elements were being discovered, but he didn't discover any of them. Nor did he discover any new scientific processes. Rather, he introduced to chemistry a new rigor, which he attributed to his studies of the Bible.

Lavoisier's research led to multiple findings. He discovered the role of oxygen in respiration as well as in combustion, and he identified sulfur as an element. He also had the opportunity to name several elements: carbon, hydrogen, and oxygen.

Antoine Lavoisier was executed during the French Revolution. It has been noted that Lavoisier kept his faith until the end. Upon the day of his death he went to the guillotine carrying a crucifix. ■

Monsieur Lavoisier and His Wife (1788) by Jacques-Louis David (1748–1825).

50 John Witherspoon Protects Religious Liberty

The colonies of the New World struggled toward freedom in their early years. Through the voice of John Witherspoon—a pastor, a university president, and a politician plotting the course toward a free republic—this struggle became heard.

As the debate regarding the necessity of the Revolutionary War pressed forward, John Witherspoon asserted that freedom was a gift from God. Influenced by his professions, Witherspoon helped to protect religious liberty and ensure appropriate separation of church and state in the founding documents of the new country. According to Witherspoon, the government should provide the assurance of freedom for all and godly people are to be actively involved in society.

As one of the Founders of the United States and one of the signers of the Declaration of Independence, Witherspoon insisted that the founding documents of the United States of America include giving thanks to God, whom Witherspoon viewed as the source and means of independence. He said, "It is by this means that the Christian may be said, in the scripture language, 'to walk with God, and to endure as seeing him who is invisible [Hebrews 11:27].'"[13] ■

Declaration of Independence (1819) by John Trumbull (1756–1843). Witherspoon is the second seated figure from the right, facing the table. The painting can be found on the back of the US $2 bill. The original hangs in the US Capitol Rotunda.

51 Adam Smith Originates Modern Economic Theory

A Scottish philosopher by trade, Adam Smith is often considered the father of modern economics and is credited with creating the notion of an "invisible hand" that governs the economy.

In his book *An Inquiry into the Nature and Causes of the Wealth of Nations*, Smith wrote, "By directing that industry in such a manner as its produce may be of the greatest value, he intends only his own gain, and he is in this, as in many other cases, led by an invisible hand to promote an end which was no part of his intention." Many of those who are familiar with Smith's writings believe that his "invisible hand" refers to God, not man.

Much of his economic theory was the result of his deep questioning of how society and economics worked. Smith said that people are motivated by self-interests, that private property should be protected, and that the role of the government should be minimized. ■

Above: 1922 printing of *An Inquiry into the Nature and Causes of the Wealth of Nations*.
Below: Manhattan Bridge under construction in 1909.

52

Robert Raikes's Sunday School Movement Reaches Orphans

Robert Raikes was the son of a newspaper publisher in Gloucester, England. After his father's death in 1757, Raikes took over as editor of the *Gloucester Journal*. He enlarged the newspaper's size and made significant improvements to its layouts. He used his newspaper to shed light on the need for social reform after observing impoverished children of his city, many of whom were orphans. These children were often forced to work twelve-hour days. On Sunday, their only day off, there was no societal structure to care for them. He observed how easy it was for them to drift into a life of crime and end up in the prison system.

Raikes, a devout Christian, could not accept this fate for these children. He believed society was failing to obey the biblical principle of aiding the "least of these" (Matthew 25:31–39). With no education, they were destined for a life of poverty. Raikes decided to establish a school on Sundays where children could learn reading, writing, and biblical concepts.

Once his Sunday schools were proven effective, Raikes distributed an article in his newspaper, which prompted approximately four thousand additional Sunday schools across England. This approach allowed for orphans to eventually transcend the injustice of abusive child labor. ■

"When the Son of Man comes in his glory, and all the angels with him, then he will sit on his glorious throne. Before him will be gathered all the nations, and he will separate people one from another as a shepherd separates the sheep from the goats. And he will place the sheep on his right, but the goats on the left. Then the King will say to those on his right, 'Come, you who are blessed by my Father, inherit the kingdom prepared for you from the foundation of the world. For I was hungry and you gave me food, I was thirsty and you gave me drink, I was a stranger and you welcomed me, I was naked and you clothed me, I was sick and you visited me, I was in prison and you came to me.'"

– Matthew 25:31–36

53 Immanuel Kant Transforms Philosophical Study

During the height of the Enlightenment in Europe, reason was supreme. Rational (provable) evidence was all that could be trusted. The idea that something could be experienced but not be measurable was inconceivable. As this pertained to faith, the order of the universe and world was proof of God. This led to faith feeling mechanical, yet as this era progressed, a split in thought began to appear. Empiricism, the theory that knowledge comes from experience, confronted rationalism. Immanuel Kant, one of the most influential philosophers in the history of Western philosophy, found a way forward that acknowledged the necessity for both ideas.

In Kant's monumental *The Critique of Pure Reason*, he argued that rational data was only knowable via empirical experience. Therefore, God would be known by both the ordered world and the human experience within it.

The Bible provides support for Kant's observations. Jeremiah 29:12–13 suggests that God is searchable and knowable rationally. If God can be found, then there must be evidence for God in the world; and, through the experience of humanity, God will be found and known. This same passage in Jeremiah references this idea by ascribing empirical (experiential) knowledge to that of the heart. Both types of knowledge are necessary, possible, and useful according to the Bible. ■

Above: Tomb of German philosopher Immanuel Kant in Königsberg Cathedral.

54 William Wilberforce Opposes British Slave Trade

Parliament member William Wilberforce spearheaded the movement in England to abolish slavery. After his conversion to Christianity in 1785, Wilberforce considered becoming a minister. He was persuaded, however, to remain in politics to advance the cause of biblical ethics. William Wilberforce understood that slavery was contrary to his understanding of what the Bible teaches, and he worked to abolish it. He wrote these words in a journal entry in 1787: "God Almighty has set before me two great objects, the suppression of the Slave Trade and the Reformation of Manners." Wilberforce's untiring efforts led Parliament to pass the Slave Trade Act of 1807, which ended slave trade that was directly connected to Britain.

> *"Let it not be said that I was silent when they needed me."*
>
> – *William Wilberforce*

Wilberforce was a member of the Clapham Sect. This subgroup within Parliament sought social changes through a series of legislative motions. Wilberforce wrote in his diary, "In the Scripture, no national crime is condemned so frequently and few so strongly as oppression and cruelty, and the not using our best endeavors to deliver our fellow-creatures from them."[14]

The efforts of Wilberforce and Clapham Sect members were highly unpopular at the time among the elites of English society. Despite this, Wilberforce's persistent efforts finally reached fruition. Just before he died, he had the satisfaction of knowing that his major life achievement, the Slavery Abolition Act of 1833, which ended slavery in most of the rest of the British Empire, was sure to become law.

During his lifetime Wilberforce also cofounded the Church Missionary Society and the Society for the Prevention of Cruelty to Animals (SPCA). ∎

Wilberforce, vintage engraved illustration, in French magazine *Le Magasin pittoresque*, 1867.

55 Former Slave Exposes Horror of Slavery

Olaudah Equiano is known as one of the most important antislavery campaigners in the history of the United Kingdom. Equiano was a West African slave who was transported to various parts of the British Empire before being freed around 1767. He had converted to Christianity in 1759, while still a slave. As a former slave, Equiano became involved in the abolition movement in Britain, working to ban slave trade in the empire. He was inspired by his own experiences and by the Zong Massacre in 1781, in which 133 slaves were thrown off a slave ship to drown.

The travesties that Equiano experienced as a slave, and his struggles later as an abolitionist, gave him cause to question his faith as a Christian on more than one occasion. He addressed this in his memoir *The Interesting Narrative of the Life of Olaudah Equiano*, which he wrote in 1789. In this book, he frequently referred to the Bible and cited biblical passages related to slavery, such as Peter and John's imprisonment after healing a beggar (Acts 4:1–3). He also compared his feelings upon being freed to Elijah being raptured up to heaven (2 Kings 2:11). ■

Left: Broadside created by British abolitionist to demonstrate the cruel crowding of a standard slave ship.
Middle: A disputed portrait of Equiano in the Royal Albert Memorial Museum, Exeter.

56 George Washington Becomes the First US President

Little is known about George Washington's childhood except for what is told through American folklore. Washington, the first president of the United States, was given the position of commander in chief by the Second Continental Congress.

Washington was generally private about his religion, but those who knew him (or of him) were aware of the Bible's influence in his life. He was often seen kneeling in prayer with an open Bible. Additionally, Washington often referred to providence and accepted whatever happened in his life or in his country as the will of providence. He attended religious services regularly and was a lay council member in his Episcopal parish. He felt that God had guided the creation of the United States and, therefore, had appointed him as president.

"If the freedom of speech is taken away then dumb and silent we may be led, like sheep to the slaughter."

– George Washington

Upon his insistence, when he was first sworn in as president on April 30, 1789, Washington took his oath of office with his hand upon a Bible. The same King James Bible he used is owned by Saint John's Freemason Lodge in New York City.

Washington remained steadfast and dedicated to his faith for his entire life. He lived by his mottos: "Deeds, not Words" and "For God and my Country."[15] ■

George Washington (ca. 1803–1805) by Gilbert Stuart (1755–1828). American painting, oil on canvas.

57 Benjamin Rush Champions Nationalized School System

Benjamin Rush—a prominent American politician, physician, and social activist—introduced the idea of a nationalized school system to the United States.

Rush suggested that the newly formed republic should require its citizens to be educated. Because the United States was a freely governed society, people needed to be able to participate intelligently in public affairs.

Rush strongly asserted that citizens of the United States should receive not only quality education but also an education that is grounded in the teachings of the Bible. Because he believed that "the Bible contains more knowledge necessary to man in his present state than any other book in the world," he argued that the Bible should be the primary means of teaching children how to read.

Along with his deep desire to see the Bible used in a prominent way within American schools, Rush also wanted the citizens of the United States to receive their education within the new nation, rather than another country. According to Rush, the principles of freedom were meant to be homegrown. He wished to extend the opportunity for a good education to all members of society, women included.

As a result, seven years after he signed America's Declaration of Independence, Rush signed the paperwork for the first college chartered in the newly formed nation of the United States of America. Initially named John and Mary's College—in honor of John Dickinson, a signer of the Constitution, and his wife, Mary Norris Dickinson, who donated much of their personal libraries to the new college—the institution was later renamed Dickinson College.

Today, Dickinson College, with its 2,400 students and 350 full-time faculty members, continues to follow the legacy of Benjamin Rush. ■

The Oldest Wooden Schoolhouse is a wooden structure located at 14 St. George Street in St. Augustine, Florida, near the city gate. It is touted as being the oldest wooden school building in the United States. The exact date of construction is unknown, but it first appears on tax records in 1716.

58 James Madison Promotes Freedom of Religion in the US Bill of Rights

The United States Constitution was adopted after the Revolutionary War at the famous Constitutional Convention in Philadelphia in 1787. The Constitution itself said very little about religion; further debate and legislation were required to determine the role religion would play in the early republic. James Madison was a key figure in this process.

In 1789 he took the lead in steering a bill through the First Federal Congress that would explicitly list the rights of American citizens, including rights regarding religion. Two years later, in 1791, ten amendments to the Constitution were ratified. Together they form the Bill of Rights—considered to be one of the most important documents for American citizens.

Madison wanted the United States to grant to its citizens the freedom of religion. This is the basis for the First Amendment: "Congress shall make no law respecting an establishment of religion, or prohibiting the free exercise thereof."

The spirit of human dignity and liberty are fundamental parts of Madison's writing and directly influenced by the Bible. In particular, the Bill of Rights reflects both 2 Corinthians 3:17, in its principles of freedom and God's protection of America, and Acts 5:29, which establishes the law of God over government and country. In this way, the Bill of Rights can be seen as an extension of the moral teachings of the Bible.

The Bill of Rights has been used to change the Constitution twenty-seven times and is still a point of debate. Regardless, its significance in America cannot be understated. ■

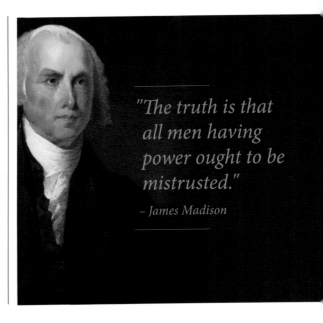

"The truth is that all men having power ought to be mistrusted."

– *James Madison*

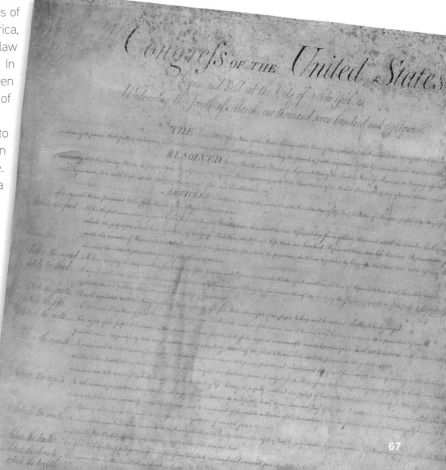

Top: *James Madison* (1821) by
Gilbert Stuart (1755–1828).
Right: The US Bill of Rights.

59

William Carey Influences the Indian Renaissance

William Carey is known as the father of modern missions. When he traveled from England to India in 1793, his arrival was a major milestone in the history of Christian missions and in the history of India.

> *"Expect great things from God, attempt great things for God."*
>
> *– William Carey*

Carey established the Serampore Mission near Calcutta on January 10, 1800. From this base, he worked for more than two decades living out the principles he valued from the Bible by treating people throughout India with compassion and dignity. As a result of his successful ministry, India was transformed.

While in India, Carey studied language, translated many dialects, and helped Bengali to emerge as a standardized written language. Carey also sought to broaden the educational system to all the castes in India.

During the time of Carey's travels, women's rights were beginning to emerge in India, and he saw a need to change societal practices. He was passionate about bringing an end to sati—the practice of a widow either throwing herself or being thrown onto the funeral pyre of her deceased husband.

Among many other issues, the burning of lepers and infanticide were also confronted by Carey. William Carey's commitment and persistence in these areas benefited the Indian society greatly. ∎

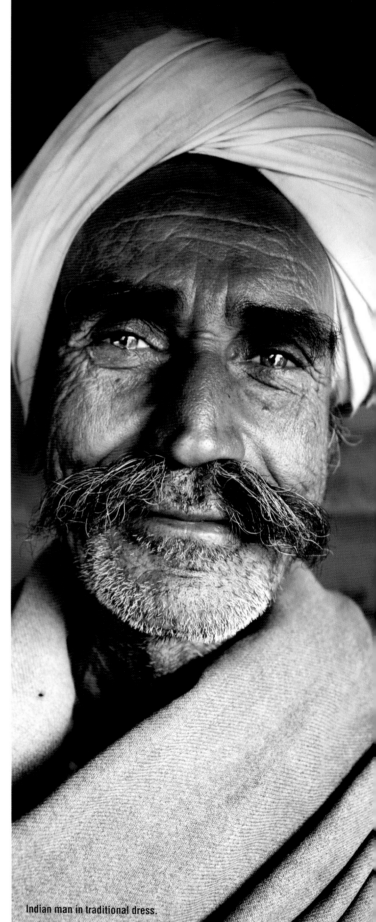

Indian man in traditional dress.

60 John Dalton Founds Modern Atomic Theory

English Quaker John Dalton was greatly influenced by his family's faith. He was able to learn to read thanks to attending a nearby Quaker school where he later taught. But despite being a teacher from the age of twelve, Dalton was not allowed to attend a British university because he was not an Anglican.

This did not stop Dalton from his continued desire to learn. He pioneered modern atomic theory in 1803, upon which quantum physics and chemistry are now based. Dalton was not the first person to come up with the idea of atoms; that dates back to ancient Greece. However, he was the first to turn it into a working, provable theory for concepts like different atomic weights for different elements. Dalton also developed gas theory and wrote the first paper suggesting that color blindness (which ran in his family) was hereditary.

Dalton's adherence to his Quaker faith and the Bible's teachings deeply affected his career, while helping to nurture his zeal for scientific knowledge. ∎

Middle: *John Dalton* (1834) by Charles Turner (1774–1857).

61 Alessandro Volta Invents the First Battery

Alessandro Volta was an Italian inventor so famous that Napoleon Bonaparte wanted him to come to France. However, Volta's shyness led him to a life of seclusion.

Volta was a lifelong Catholic who fended off accusations that he lacked faith because he believed in "supernatural grace" as much as in the rationality of science. He cited the teachings of Jesus as a particular guidance in his life and regularly attended Mass. His family wanted him to study for the clergy, and he nearly became a Jesuit before turning to a career as a professor of physics.

Volta's decision to choose physics led

to something quite exciting: the creation of the first battery in 1800. The invention was spurred on by a disagreement with rival Luigi Galvani. Galvani believed electricity was derived only from animals, alive or dead. Volta proved him wrong by creating a purely inorganic battery out of wine goblets. From this he created the Voltaic Pile—the first electrical battery that could continuously provide an electric current to a circuit.

Volta's discovery led to significant breakthroughs by other scientists because it demonstrated a practical and reliable way to produce electricity. ■

Top: Reconstruction of the first battery invented by Alessandro Volta.
Bottom: Alessandro Volta (1745–1827), demonstrating his electricity-generating apparatus to Napoleon.

62 Elizabeth Fry Initiates Prison Reform

Humane standards *for the treatment of prisoners,* especially women, were instituted due to the work of Elizabeth Fry in nineteenth-century England. Upon encountering the prison system in the 1800s, Fry was horrified at the overcrowding, starvation, hopelessness, and suffering of the prisoners. Sadly, the children of female inmates were often forced to endure the same fate as their mothers, adding to the problem.

"It is an honor to appear on the side of the afflicted." – Elizabeth Fry

Elizabeth was raised in a Quaker home and was a Quaker minister. She was influenced by American Quaker William Savery's messages to fight the issues of poverty and injustice. Fry read the Bible to inmates and taught them to sew in order to give them a way to earn a living when they were released.

Fry's work with prison reform resulted in the passing of the Prison Reform Act of 1823 in the House of Commons, which ultimately led to regulation of prisons on a national basis. Additionally, she took her prison reform ideas to several countries in Europe. ∎

63

Michael Faraday Contributes to Electromagnetism and Electrochemistry

Few scientists have contributed more to the investigation of electromagnetism and electrochemistry than English physicist and chemist Michael Faraday. His many discoveries and achievements, including principles behind the electric motor and field theory, set him among the greatest men of his time. Faraday's nearly 400 publications, including twenty-five years of papers known as "Experimental Researches in Electricity," established his reputation as an effective communicator of science.

Faraday was also known as a biblical literalist. He viewed God's creation as a perfect machine. In his manuscript *Matter*, Faraday wrote, "God has been pleased to work in his material creation by laws, and these laws are made evident to us by the constancy of the characters of matter and the constancy of the effects which it produces."[16]

Faraday's approaches to religion and science were distinct from those of his peers. He wrote to Ada Lovelace, "I am of a small and despised sect of Christians, known, if known at all, as Sandemanians, and our hope is founded on the faith that is in Christ." As for science, he adhered to what Cantor referred to as "scriptural physics." Rather than follow the natural theology of his day, Faraday believed in a theology of nature similar to the concept of God's presence in nature that was also espoused by Newton. ∎

Michael Faraday (ca. 1852), daguerreotype by Matthew Brady (1822–1896).

64 Lord Shaftesbury Enacts Social Reforms

Antony Ashley Cooper, known as Lord Shaftesbury, believed that failure to do good for others was a terrible sin. Having been born into an age of reform, matters of faith were important to him.

As a child he was influenced by the family's housekeeper, Maria Millis, who told him Bible stories and taught him the importance of loving other people. His religion spurred him to become involved with the world, and his faith was a priority in his life. In his diary Shaftesbury once meditated on James 4:17: "Therefore, to him who knows to do good and does not do it, to him it is sin" (NKJV).

Lord Shaftesbury answered a call to public service as a British politician and philanthropist. His efforts to alleviate the injustices caused by the Industrial Revolution included, among other things, reforms that banned employment of women and children in coal mines, provided care for the mentally ill, and established

> *"By everything true, everything holy, you are your brother's keeper."*
> – *Lord Shaftesbury*

the limit of a ten-hour day for factory workers. He went on to fight for millers, miners, chimney sweeps, child laborers, and the uneducated poor.

In taking seriously the biblical principle to "do good," Lord Shaftesbury enacted many social reforms that had a tremendous impact on the world during his lifetime. The great preacher C. H. Spurgeon eulogized him: "We have, in my judgment, lost the best man of the age."[17] Georgina Battiscombe wrote, "No man has in fact ever done more to lessen the extent of human misery or to add to the sum total of human happiness."[18] ∎

65 André-Marie Ampère
Pioneers Electrodynamics

French physicist André-Marie Ampère was a pioneer in the science of electrodynamics. Ampère developed concepts regarding the relationships between electricity and magnetism in his major work *Memoir on the Mathematical Theory of Electrodynamic Phenomena*. The measurement of an electrical current, ampere, is named after him.

Ampère often repeated that the three greatest markers in his life were his first Communion, reading of the "Eulogy of Descartes" by Antoine Leonard Thomas, and the fall of the Bastille. Early in his life, he devoured works such as *The Imitation of Christ* by Thomas à Kempis and the expansive *Encyclopédie* edited by Denis Diedert and Jean Le Rond d'Alembert, which contained both skeptical and orthodox theological articles. At times, Ampère's personal faith in God wavered. But Antoine-Frédéric Ozanam wrote that later in life "the religious doubts and struggles of his early life had ceased."

Ampère believed that the works of the creator give rise to knowledge of the creator himself: "Heaven and earth are full of your glory!" He once told Ozanam, "How great God is! All our knowledge is absolutely nothing." ■

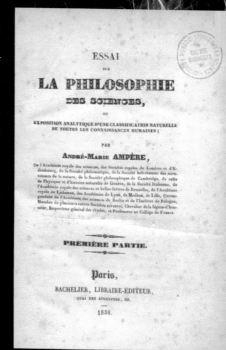

"Ordinarily logic is divided into the examination of ideas, judgments, arguments, and methods. The two latter are generally reduced to judgments, that is, arguments are reduced to apodictic judgments that such and such conclusions follow from such and such premises, and method is reduced to judgments that prescribe the procedure that should be followed in the search for truth." – André-Marie Ampère

"Revival is a renewed conviction of sin and repentance, followed by an intense desire to live in obedience to God." – Charles G. Finney

(66

The Second Great Awakening Reshapes a Nation

Revivalism and camp meetings had tremendous influence on nineteenth-century America. In his *Lectures on Revivals in Religion*, Presbyterian preacher Charles Finney indicated that the purpose of a religious revival is "the more or less general awakening of all classes, and insuring attention to the claims of God."

The Second Great Awakening, a reprise of the Great Awakening of the early 1800s, was a revival movement that swept across America, characterized by enthusiastic camp meetings in which large crowds gathered for days or weeks of praying, singing, and preaching. One of the most important of these was the Cane Ridge Revival in 1801, which drew more than 10,000 people to sparsely populated northeastern Kentucky. Although the influence of the Second Great Awakening was mostly in frontier areas, it also spread east due to the evangelism efforts of Charles Finney.

The revival continued in waves through the 1830s. Groups such as the American Bible Society (founded in 1816) brought the Bible's influence to ever-larger segments of the American population. Some preachers addressed the injustices of slavery. Finney and others openly encouraged black slaves to seek their freedom.

Because of these revival meetings, widely-dispersed settlers throughout the region were able to come together and worship God. Additionally, the active revival culture gave rise to dialogue about reform issues such as temperance, slavery, and charity for the poor. These camp meetings were a catalyst for many individual conversions, as well as reshaping society on the frontier.

During the 1840s, the widespread revival fervor cooled off and the Second Great Awakening effectively died out. But church affiliation across the United States remained at high levels for decades. ∎

Top Left: Lithograph of revival (ca. 1794).
Left: Line art drawing of Charles Finney.

67 George Mueller Cares for Abandoned Children

Bible passages such as Colossians 3:12–13 command followers of Jesus to act with "compassionate hearts, kindness, humility, meekness, and patience, bearing with one another." This type of sentiment changed George Mueller's life from one of selfishness to one of extraordinary sacrifice and compassion.

Prior to his religious conversion, Mueller lived as a wholehearted skeptic. He was often critical of Christians, drunk, and obnoxious enough for the local police to know him. When he encountered a group that studied the Bible, George recognized something lacking in his life. He then dedicated his life to studying the Bible and living the principles found within its pages.

Much later, after leaving his native Prussia, he became a pastor in England. Mueller was unnerved at the number of orphaned and abandoned children in the streets. Without the means to begin, he established an orphanage that would eventually care for more than 10,000 children. ▪

John Quincy Adams Wins Freedom for African Slaves in the *Amistad* Supreme Court Case

The 1841 United States Supreme Court *Amistad* case decided whether a group of captured Africans could be legally recognized as slaves in the United States. The Africans, who had been sent by the Spanish to work on plantations in Cuba, escaped from their chains while onboard the Spanish ship *Amistad*. When they were captured by the US Navy and brought to Connecticut, a massive legal challenge began.

Abolitionist forces recruited former president John Quincy Adams to defend the Africans. He won the case; the Supreme Court ruled in the Africans' favor.

As a thank-you to Adams, the Africans gave him a Bible and a note of thanks, which includes the words of Psalm 124:

> Most Respected Sir,—The Mendi people give thanks for all your kindness to them. They will never forget your defence of their rights before the great court at Washington. They feel that they owe to you, in a large measure, their deliverance from the Spaniards, and from slavery or death. They will pray for you as long as you live, Mr. Adams. . . . Mr. Adams, we want to make you a present of a beautiful bible! Will you please to accept it, and when you look at it, or read it, remember your poor and grateful clients? We read in this holy book, "If it had not been the Lord who was on our side, when men rose up against us, then they had swallowed us up quick, when their wrath was kindled against us. Blessed be the Lord, who hath not given us a prey to their teeth. Our soul is escaped as a bird out of the snare of the fowler; the snare is broken and we are escaped. Our help is in the name of the Lord, who made Heaven and Earth."[19] ∎

John Quincy Adams (ca. 1847), daguerreotype by Matthew Brady (1822–1896).

69

Samuel Morse's First Telegraph Message Acknowledges God

The son of a Christian minister, Samuel Morse held a high view of God's sovereignty. He recognized that his talents and gifts were a means through which God's name could be honored.

Morse was educated at Yale, where he studied philosophy and mathematics. A highly skilled realist painter, Morse became interested in electronic communication almost by happenstance. While he was in Washington, DC, having been commissioned for a painting, he received tragic news—his wife had died. Returning home to Boston in grief, Morse resolved

to invent a means by which communication could travel faster than the legs of a horse.

With a patient trust in God's sovereignty and a firm conviction that the principles found in the Bible could be spread through various means, Morse successfully invented a cheap and versatile single-wire telegraph. He was also instrumental in inventing the universal language of the telegraph now named after him: Morse code. The line was officially opened in 1844 with a transmission from the Supreme Court to the US Capitol containing the following biblical quote: "What hath God wrought" (Number 23:23, KJV). ∎

"Education without religion is in danger of substituting wild theories for the simple commonsense rules of Christianity." – Samuel Morse

Top: Old Morse key.
Middle: *Samuel F. B. Morse*, steel engraving by John Sartain (1808–1897).

70

Frederick Douglass Works to Abolish Slavery

Although Frederick Douglass was born a slave, he was taught to read, to write, and to study the Bible. Douglass eventually found freedom in Massachusetts, where he flourished as a gifted scholar and public speaker. He was recruited to join the Massachusetts Anti-Slavery Society. It was here that he became an influential voice in the fight against slavery and for human rights, and he also held several positions within the federal government. Douglass even advised President Abraham Lincoln when he wrote the Emancipation Proclamation (1863), which declared all slaves in Southern states to be free.

Douglass learned about the value of freedom from his study of the Bible. This moved him to action in working to help free victims of slavery. He argued that slavery should be abolished completely and in all circumstances, and he considered the brand of Christianity that endorsed slavery to be hypocritical and unbiblical. Douglass's efforts helped to lead the United States out of some of its darkest days. ∎

1855 portrait of Frederick Douglass (1818–1895), former slave and abolitionist.

71

Charles Dickens Inspires Social Reform

At odds with organized religion, Charles Dickens advocated for the oppressed while cultivating his own private faith and study of the Bible. As a child, he experienced the darker side of nineteenth-century British life. His father was placed in debtor's prison, which forced young Dickens to work for twelve hours per day, six days per week. He saw how the rich were seemingly enjoying life while the destitute had little hope for transcending oppression.

"I have been bent and broken, but —I hope—into a better shape."

– Charles Dickens

After his father was released from prison, Dickens finished his education and became a reporter. Eventually, Dickens began writing novels. Spurred on by ideas about child labor reform and humane treatment of people, Dickens used his writing skills to help make a difference. He wrote pamphlets and other articles about social reform, and his novels like *Oliver Twist* powerfully and vividly illustrated the issues.

Dickens soon became recognized as one of the most important writers of the nineteenth century. His book *A Tale of Two Cities* is the best-selling novel of all time. Set in London and Paris during the French Revolution, it showed both the desperate plight of the French peasantry, as well as the terrible excesses that followed the overthrow of the aristocracy. The plot is an echo of a pervasive biblical theme: the power of individual sacrifice to bring redemption to others.

In his very personal manuscript *The Life of Our Lord,* Dickens outlined his private faith in God for his children. In his will, Dickens attributed the Bible as his source of inspiration: "I exhort my dear children humbly to try to guide themselves by the teaching of the New Testament in its broad spirit, and to put no faith in any man's narrow construction of its letter here or there." ∎

Although men like Charles Dickens fought for the humane treatment of child laborers, the practice of child labor persisted also in America. The photo above depicts child laborers as portrayed by Lewis Hine in 1911. Dust-covered breaker boys at Pennsylvania coal mines used hammers to "clean" the coal, separating slate rock from the mined coal.

72 Lord Kelvin Develops Laws of Thermodynamics

Scottish-Irish scientist William Thomson, who became known as Lord Kelvin, was born in Belfast, Ireland. Kelvin, who was always on time to weekly chapel, remained a faithful Scotch Presbyterian throughout his life. Lord Kelvin's understanding of the providence and rule of God was not just a private matter reserved for Sundays alone, though. He saw God's providential work in all things, including the ordering of nature.

Kelvin worked as a physicist and engineer at the University of Glasgow, where he was instrumental in the synthesis of the diverse disciplines. With the rising sciences of geology and biological evolution, Kelvin's trust in God helped guide his scientific findings, leading him to conclude that earth's old age meant that it was not developed by blind processes, which he deduced would have taken too long to evolve without the guidance of a creator. These insights led to an understanding of biological evolution and diversity called theistic evolution.

Most people link Kelvin's work to his ability to merge his religious convictions and scientific curiosity in what is today called modern physics. Kelvin is primarily known for developing the first and second laws of thermodynamics.

Kelvin, a man of profound faith in God with a vigorous scientific mind, was buried at Westminster Abbey, near the grave of Sir Isaac Newton. ∎

"If you study science deep enough and long enough, it will force you to believe in God."

– *Lord Kelvin*

One application of the second law of thermodynamics is that heat transfers naturally from a hotter object to a colder object but does not spontaneously transfer from cold to hot.

Above: William Thomson, Lord Kelvin.

73 Louis Pasteur Investigates Germs and Invents Life-Saving Vaccines

In the 1800s, people believed that life appeared spontaneously—that fleas grew from dust or maggots from dead flesh. Frenchman Louis Pasteur, a devout Catholic and meticulous scientist, was not convinced of this randomness.

For Pasteur, all life had a point of origin. In the Bible's book of Genesis he saw a description of the creation of the universe illustrating that life is not a product of nothingness but rather the work of an intelligent, logical creator. This concept of life's origins caused him to think it impossible that disease could come about randomly.

Pasteur began his research by exploring the causes of disease via testing for differences in organic material. Some samples were stored in the open air. Others were sealed from the environment. He learned that only the exposed material produced the growth of harmful elements. His experiment showed that food went bad because of contamination by microbes in the air. He went on to argue that these could cause disease. His groundbreaking germ theory led to the development of antiseptics and changed health care forever.

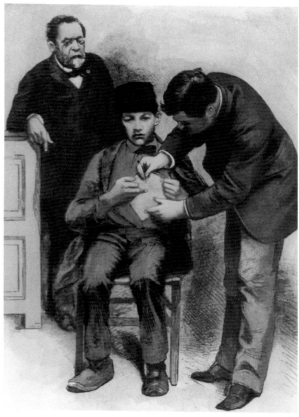

This discovery also led Pasteur to develop the process of pasteurizing milk and to invent the first vaccines for anthrax and rabies, among others. His work, when joined to the work of Robert Koch, led to the understanding that we have today regarding germs and bacteria. Because of Pasteur's Bible-influenced contribution to science, disease and unnecessary death are more easily preventable. ■

Milk pasteurization system is shown at a food and drink exhibition. Pasteurization uses heat to kill bacteria in food and drink.

Top: Rabies virus hydrophobia vaccination being given to teenage Jean-Baptiste Jupille at the Pasteur laboratory in October 1885.

74   Clara Barton Founds the Red Cross

During the American Civil War, Clara Barton was dissatisfied with the ineffective care of soldiers. Based on the Bible's teachings about the importance of caring for others, Barton was determined that more could be done to care for these men. After a persistent series of pleas, she was given permission to begin.

Barton worked vigorously, orchestrating the supply of medical supplies, food, blankets, and medical care for American soldiers. She often placed herself near to the battlefield conflicts to maximize the availability of medical help. When the war ended, she continued her assistance. She established an office to aid the identification of prisoners, deceased soldiers, and those buried in unmarked graves.

After the war, Barton visited Europe, where she obtained permission from the Red Cross in Switzerland to establish an American Red Cross. Over time, the scope of the Red Cross was expanded to include disaster relief for flooding and famine.

Clara Barton's dedication and persistence carried the intent of the Bible into the midst of harm's way for the benefit of many. She continued humanitarian work in this spirit into her nineties. ■

Top: Red Cross workers clear the wreckage after a fire and explosion in Manhattan's East Village.
Above: US field hospital in Saint-Hilaire-Petitville, east of Carentan, France.

75 Victor Hugo Draws on Biblical Themes in His Writings

Victor Hugo (1802–1885), a novelist and playwright, frequently drew upon biblical themes in his writings. He often expressed admiration for the Bible, particularly for its literary qualities. In one chapter of his famous novel *Les Misérables* (1862), Hugo conveys admiration for John's writing in Revelation:

> We need not speak of the immense exile of Patmos who, on his part also, overwhelms the real world with a protest in the name of the ideal world, who makes of his vision an enormous satire and casts on Rome-Nineveh, on Rome-Babylon, on Rome-Sodom, the flaming reflection of the Apocalypse. John on his rock is the sphinx on its pedestal; we may understand him, he is a Jew, and it is Hebrew. ∎

Cosette Sweeping (1862) by Émile Bayard (1837–1891), original illustration from *Les Misérables*.

(76 Abraham Lincoln Signs the Emancipation Proclamation

Born into a poor family living on America's western frontier in Hodgenville, Kentucky, in 1809, Abraham Lincoln was a determined and precocious young man with a mild temperament and a witty candor. Essentially self-educated, young Lincoln had several favorite books that he read and reread, including Daniel Defoe's *Robinson Crusoe* and the King James Bible.

He became a successful lawyer before launching his political career in the 1840s. Lincoln's upbringing exposed him to the teachings of the Bible, and throughout his life he was readily able to draw from his commanding knowledge of the Bible—he would quote verses from memory in the most astounding moments.

Long before he became America's sixteenth president, Lincoln argued against the Kansas-Nebraska Act of 1854. The act permitted citizens of these two newly forming states to vote on whether slavery should be permitted in their territories. Stephen A. Douglas, the act's designer, ended up losing in the 1860 presidential election against Lincoln.

Lincoln firmly believed that every human reflects the image of God, based on Genesis 1:27 and other biblical passages. In a speech in Lewiston, Illinois, on August 17, 1858, Lincoln upheld the Declaration of Independence's view that "all men are created equal." Lincoln argued that this "noble understanding of the justice of the Creator to His creatures" should be applied to all people. These principles and proclamations, he argued, were a "beacon" to guide later generations. America's bloodiest conflict in history, the American Civil War, was fought in large part over the slavery issue.

Lincoln later declared, "And upon this act, sincerely believed to be an act of justice, warranted by the Constitution, upon military necessity, I invoke the considerate judgment of mankind, and the gracious favor of Almighty God." This was the immortal conclusion to his bold and courageous document known as the Emancipation Proclamation, which Lincoln signed into effect on January 1, 1863, declaring that slaves in America were "then, thenceforward, and forever free."

By sticking to his biblically based principles and boldly facing dangerous opposition, Lincoln stands as a solid example of someone profoundly influenced by the Bible. With regard to the Emancipation Proclamation, Lincoln remarked, "I never, in my life, felt more certain that I was doing right, than I do in signing this paper." His conviction paid off, as the Emancipation Proclamation was a major catalyst for the congressional approval of the Thirteenth Amendment, which officially outlawed slavery from the Union. ∎

Left: Abraham Lincoln.

77

"In God We Trust" Added to US Coins and Paper Currency

The Founders of the United States were in tune with the workings of providence throughout the birth of the nation. Reflecting on the success of the American Revolutionary War, Washington stated, "The hand of Providence has been so conspicuous in all this."[20] From the genesis of the nation to the evangelical revivals known as the First and Second Great Awakenings, Americans were often profoundly affected by itinerant preachers—who passionately carried their Bibles in their hands and the knowledge of its teachings in their hearts.

By the time of the American Civil War, religious sentiment was at an all-time high—led by the unwavering and prescient leadership of Abraham Lincoln and his trust in the providence of God. In a letter dated November 20, 1861, Secretary of the Treasury Salmon P. Chase urged James Pollock, director of the Mint in Philadelphia, "Dear Sir: No nation can be strong except in the strength of God, or safe except in His defense. The trust of our people in God should be declared on our national coins." In 1864, the first coins were minted bearing the inscription "In God We Trust."

Nearly a century later, in 1955, President Dwight D. Eisenhower signed a law that made it mandatory for all US currency to also bear this inscription. Subsequently, by 1957 the motto "In God We Trust" was stamped on all paper currency as well. ■

78

William Booth Founds the Salvation Army to Assist the Poor

William Booth was a British pastor who began his ministry in 1852. Dissatisfied with how his church superiors treated the poor and needy, he took his understanding of the Bible's principles to London's streets, starting with a series of evangelical missions in 1865. He had the idea of creating an army of the destitute, redeeming lost souls and even petty criminals. The inspiration was found in the New Testament stories about Jesus spending time with tax collectors and prostitutes.

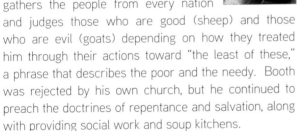

Booth and his wife were also inspired by the parable of the sheep and the goats in Matthew 25:31–46, in which a king (believed by many to be Jesus) gathers the people from every nation and judges those who are good (sheep) and those who are evil (goats) depending on how they treated him through their actions toward "the least of these," a phrase that describes the poor and the needy. Booth was rejected by his own church, but he continued to preach the doctrines of repentance and salvation, along with providing social work and soup kitchens.

The name *Salvation Army* stems from the concept of an army in one of Booth's letters from 1878. First calling them a "Volunteer Army" or "God's Army," Booth energized his ministry by calling his down-and-out followers a "Salvation Army." He adapted a military structure into the ministry, establishing himself as "General" over the "soldiers." His Salvation Army surged in popularity, and its effective ministry in social relief among the needy made Booth well known as "the prophet of the poor."[21]

Originally confined to London's East Side, Salvation Army missions soon spread throughout the British Empire and later to the United States, Canada, Europe, and Latin America. ∎

Above: Salvation Army officer collects donations.
Below: Salvation Army lassies giving sweets to two soldiers of the 351st Field Artillery.

Top: William Booth, founder of the Salvation Army.

John D. Rockefeller Establishes Faith-Based Philanthropy

John D. Rockefeller was a businessman who was exceptionally good at making money. His careful yet hard-driving ways produced the massive Standard Oil Company. He was also a devout Christian. John credited his mother as a key influence in instilling in him the value of charity. Rockefeller was open about his Christian faith and high view of the Bible. He said, "We are never too old to study the Bible. Each time the lessons are studied comes some new meaning, some new thought which will make us better."[22]

Rockefeller's combination of tremendous wealth and commitment to charity set the standard for philanthropy in America. Rockefeller's generous contributions benefited hospitals, institutions of higher education, and local churches. But it was the creation of the Rockefeller Foundation that carries the influence of Bible-inspired charity into nearly every segment of society to this day. ■

Grand Teton National Park united with the Jackson Hole National Monument (donated by Rockefeller) on September 14, 1950 to become the present-day Grand Teton National Park.

80 Guglielmo Marconi Develops the Radio Telegraph System

In the attic of his Italian home in the 1890s, Guglielmo Marconi was hard at work. He successfully created the first wireless telegraph, forever changing the way the world communicates. Signor Marconi's "magic box" would save lives and bring continents together.

As a self-taught amateur, Marconi worked diligently to develop the radio telegraph system. He also attended lectures by great science communicator Michael Faraday and worked closely with mentor Augusto Righi in local physics laboratories.

At the start of his experiments, he worked to transmit electromagnetic waves across the room. He knew he had succeeded in transmitting the invisible waves when he was able to connect with his brother Alfonso, who was beyond a distant hill. Eventually, Marconi's radio signals also crossed oceans and sailed into deep space.

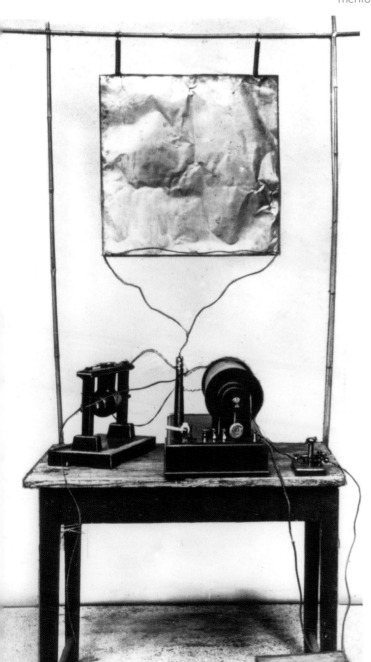

"I am proud to be a Christian. I believe not only as a Christian, but as a scientist as well. A wireless device can deliver a message through the wilderness. In prayer the human spirit can send invisible waves to eternity, waves that achieve their goal in front of God."

– Guglielmo Marconi

Marconi wrote that his science was "an expression of the Supreme Will, which aims at bringing people closer to each other in order to help them better understand and improve themselves."[23] He believed that just as prayer can send invisible waves to God, so "a wireless device can deliver a message through the wilderness."[24] ■

Above: Guglielmo Marconi.
Left: A replica of one of the first radio transmitters, a spark-gap transmitter, built by Guglielmo Marconi in August 1895 during his development of radio communication. It generated radio waves by an electric spark between two electrodes of a Righi spark gap (left, on table).

81

Oxyrhynchus Papyri Are Discovered in Egypt

Discovered in Egypt in the nineteenth and twentieth centuries, the Oxyrhynchus Papyri are among the most incredible manuscript collections ever found. Thousands of papyrus scraps dating from the first to sixth centuries AD preserve works of the greatest Greek poets, fragments of ancient science, and pieces of Roman history texts. The papyri were discovered in an ancient garbage dump near the town once known as Oxyrhynchus.

Among the many papyri containing classics of the ancient world, a number of biblical texts were discovered—including scraps of the Gospels, sections of very early noncanonical gospels, hymns, prayers, letters, and pieces of the Hebrew Bible. The earliest New Testament papyri in the collection are dated to the mid-second century.

The Oxyrhynchus Papyri provide us with a unique glimpse into the lives of literate, educated people who highly valued the written word. In a world with no printing presses, the laborious work of copying texts took hours or days and required a lot of skill and expense. Today, books are everyday items, but in the ancient world, written texts were luxury items. To the people of Oxyrhynchus, biblical texts were obviously every bit as significant as the texts of the greatest poets, dramatists, and scientists of the ancient world. ■

82

Amy Carmichael Rescues Girls and Women in India

Amy Carmichael, an Irish woman who served for over five decades as a missionary in India, rescued thousands of girls and young women from forced temple prostitution. In 1901 she founded an orphanage and a mission, the Dohnavur Fellowship. This organization continues to help children in India today.

Deeply moved by the plight of Indian children, especially girls, Carmichael (1867–1951) worked tirelessly to help them. She sacrificed her own safety, often receiving threats, and traveled long distances to save children from a life of slavery.

Reflecting on the words of Acts 20:35, Amy wrote:

Have you ever wondered who remembered and told St. Paul that lovely word of our Lord, which no one records in the Gospels? We can picture the sorrowful people standing on the shore listening to it, and treasuring it in their hearts.

Paul had been speaking of ordinary work and of working so that we may have something to give. But perhaps there was a further thought in his mind. The people wanted to keep him. Others needed him. We are not here to enjoy one another. Love must not be selfish. Love, the truest, deepest kind of love, gives and goes on giving—like the sea upon whose shore they stood together.

It is more blessed (more very happy) to give than to receive. He who knew all kinds of happiness said that. So it must be true. It is true. ■

Above Left: *Gospel of Matthew.* Discovered by Bernard Pyne Grenfell and Arthur Hunt in Oxyrhynchus, 1897.

Above: Amy Carmichael with children in India.

83 Henri Dunant Receives the First Nobel Peace Prize

The book *A Memory of Solferino* helped launch the International Committee of the Red Cross, and its author, Henri Dunant, received the first Nobel Peace Prize in 1901. Henri's exposure to the needs of the destitute began early on. His father was the head of an institution for orphans, and his mother visited the poor and the sick.

Dunant grew up in Switzerland at a time when the spirit of awakening was strong. A great influence in his life was an evangelical preacher at Collège Calvin in Geneva named Louis Gaussen. Dunant and his family joined the socially minded Church of the Awakening to better live by the principles that helped guide them. Dunant also joined the Geneva Society for Alms at age eighteen and later founded the Geneva chapter of the YMCA.

Later in life, Dunant reflected on the horrors he witnessed at the battle of Solferino and what compelled him to diligently work to provide aid to people in need: "I was, as it were, lifted out of myself, compelled by some higher power and inspired by the breath of God." He also shared, "I was aware of an intuition, vague and yet profound, that my work was an instrument of His Will."[26]

After Dunant's passing, a Red Cross chairman wrote, "Dunant's grave is in Zurich, but his memorial is the worldwide Red Cross." His belief in what he did and the purpose behind it is part of the Red Cross's mission to this day. ∎

Top: Nobel Prize.
Above: Henry Dunant.

84 Albert Schweitzer Treats the Sick and Preaches the Bible in Africa

One of the most prominent humanitarians of the twentieth century, Albert Schweitzer (1875–1965) left behind his opportunities for a successful career in Europe to serve the people of Africa.

He and his wife, Helene, arrived in Lambaréné (now in Gabon) in 1913 and started a clinic in an old chicken coop. They often traveled long distances under arduous conditions to treat their patients, many of whom suffered from severe health problems, including dysentery, malaria, sleeping sickness, and nicotine poisoning.

Schweitzer also frequently preached to congregations on Sunday mornings, often changing details from stories in the Bible so the people would more readily understand his message. In one of his sermons on the apostle Paul, Schweitzer speaks of Paul wearing a loincloth and working as a maker of mats (rather than a maker of tents) in order to better connect with his audience:

> First, he walked by foot for many, many years, going from one village to another. Then, after he earned some money by making mats, he went on a boat to some other cities. Sometimes people were good to him, "Come into our hut! Eat with us!" At other times they were wicked toward him. Then they said, "What does he want, this pauper who doesn't even have a decent loincloth? He wants to preach us the truth!" So they took stones and threw them at him, and, in this way, several times, they almost killed him.[27]

Schweitzer served nearly fifty years as a missionary doctor in Africa. He was awarded the Nobel Peace Prize in 1953 and died in Lambaréné in 1965 at the age of ninety. ■

85 Woodrow Wilson Creates the Fourteen Points of Peace

Woodrow Wilson, the son of a Presbyterian minister, was a man of strong conviction. Upon becoming the twenty-eighth president of the United States, he used his platform many times to speak on behalf of the Bible. He said, "The Bible (with its individual value of the human soul) is undoubtedly the book that has made democracy." To Wilson, the Bible was his foundation. He used the Bible to guide not only his life but also his decisions as a US president.

Wilson kept the United States out of the Great War for as long as possible. Eventually, President Wilson recognized that going to war could not be avoided, but he did not want any lives to end in vain. Focusing on a peaceful resolve was a priority. This was the onset of the creation of the Fourteen Points of Peace, a plan that many skeptics viewed as too optimistic and progressive.

The Fourteen Points of Peace was meant to create peace, freedom, and stability in the world in the wake of its bloodiest war to date. This desire was not accepted by America, and Wilson's ideals were not well received. Still, this wartime president advocated for biblical principles of peace. Although the United States was not interested in supporting Wilson's vision for peace on earth and soon entered World War II, Wilson's legacy as president will be forever marked by his efforts. ∎

"The ear of the leader must ring with the voices of the people."

– Woodrow Wilson

Above: President Woodrow Wilson throwing out the first ball, opening day, 1916.

86

George Washington Carver Unlocks Peanut's Potential

Born into slavery, George Washington Carver overcame seemingly insurmountable odds and social barriers on his way to becoming a brilliant scientist, botanist, chemist, and inventor who studied and worked at Tuskegee University.

Everything Carver did was inspired by the Bible. On January 21, 1921, while speaking to the United States House on how to use the peanut to improve the Southern economy, Carver stated, "If you go to the first chapter of Genesis, we can interpret very clearly what God intended. Behold I give you every herb that bears seed. To you it shall be meat."[28] To Carver, this Bible passage revealed the potential of what he could do with the peanut to help others be lifted from poverty—particularly, the struggling African American farmers.

While at Tuskegee, Carver single-handedly changed the South's agricultural reliance on cotton. Additionally, he helped to improve the living conditions of many African Americans.

Carver's reputation as a man of faith, frugality, humbleness, and generosity is well noted. His epitaph reads: "He could have added fortune to fame, but caring for neither, he found happiness and honor in being helpful to the world." ∎

Right: George Washington Carver (front row, center) poses with fellow staff members at the Tuskegee Institute (now known as Tuskegee University) located in the US state of Alabama.

87 Dorothy Day Cofounds the Catholic Worker Movement

From the story of the fish and loaves found in John 6 in the Bible comes a movement of workers dedicated to human rights, justice, and peace. Dorothy Day, who once was a spunky socialist, became a devoted Catholic. She was impressed with the small gesture of the boy whose bread and fish were used to feed more than five thousand people. In that story, Jesus takes the boy's five loaves of bread and two fish and is able to feed the gathered masses.

Day cofounded the Catholic Worker Movement, believing their work could make a positive impact on issues of social justice. When it came to discussing her Christian faith and life's purpose, Day wrote, "What we do is very little, but it's like the little boy with a few loaves

"They cannot see that we must lay one brick at a time, take one step at a time." – Dorothy Day

and fishes. Christ took that little and increased it. He will do the rest."[29]

Day's efforts set a precedent that has carried on into modern society in the Catholic Worker Movement, which continues to work toward peace and justice. Throughout its history, members of this movement have taken key roles in government, journalism, universities, labor unions, and all across public life. ■

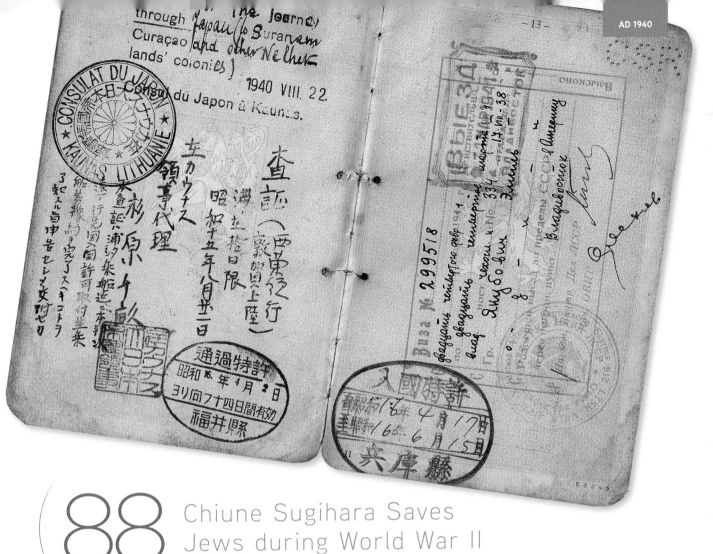

88 Chiune Sugihara Saves Jews during World War II

Sometimes called "the Japanese Schindler," Chiune Sugihara saved the lives of up to 10,000 Jews during World War II. As the vice-consul of the Japanese consulate in Kaunas, Lithuania, Sugihara was deeply affected by the plight of the Jewish refugees in the country.

Sugihara's wife, Yukiko, was moved to help the Jews after reading the biblical book of Lamentations, a collection of sorrowful poems about the destruction of Jerusalem. She encouraged her husband to take action in assisting the Jews.

Sugihara began handwriting hundreds, and eventually thousands, of visas to help Jews cross the border to safety. Writing these visas was not only unauthorized but also dangerous. Sugihara had a decision to make: accept and follow the government's decisions that directly violated biblical principles or break the law in order to show compassion to people in need. Sugihara knew his conscience was telling him he had to do something about the injustices being imposed on the Jews. He explained, "I may have to disobey my government, but if I don't I will be disobeying God."[30]

Defying both his superiors and his need for sleep, he spent eighteen to twenty hours a day in the summer of 1940 writing travel visas for as many Jews as he could, before he was reassigned to a consulate in Berlin. In 1945 Soviet troops imprisoned Sugihara and his family in a POW camp in Romania, where they remained until they were able to return to Japan in 1946.

In 1985, Israel named Sugihara one of the Righteous Among the Nations, an honor given to non-Jews who risked their lives to save Jews during the Holocaust. He is the only Japanese citizen to have received the honor, which provides each recipient with a medal, a certificate of honor, and honorary citizenship of the State of Israel. ■

Above: 1940-issued transit visa by vice-consul Sugihara in Lithuania. The Czech holder of the passport escaped to Poland in 1939 and then to Lithuania. He used his visa from Sugihara to travel through Siberia to China.

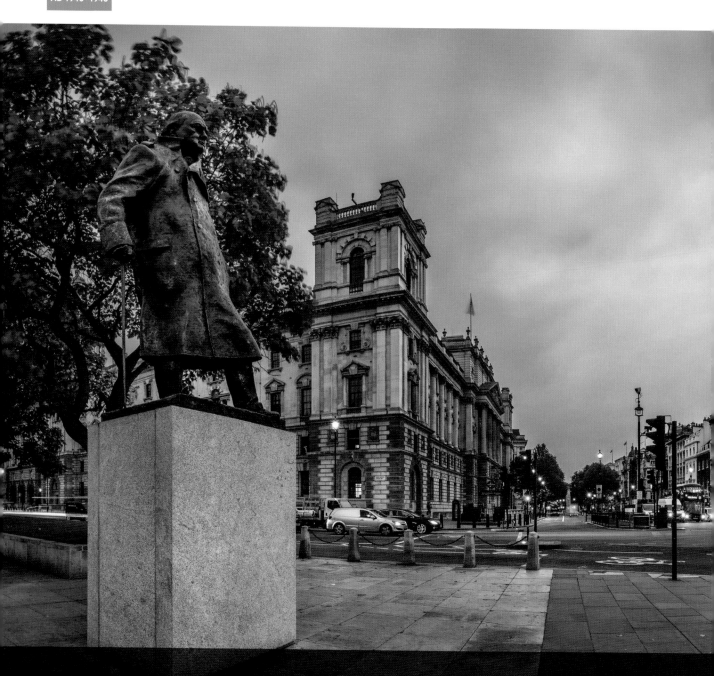

World War II was an extremely turbulent time in Great Britain as the Nazi regime was quickly taking over most of the European continent. Churchill was determined that Britain would not cower to the Nazis, and he urged the citizens of England to get behind him to fight nobly.

Anglicanism was a common thread that most all the English shared in some way, so Churchill used the religion of the people to bind them to his cause of holding off the Nazis. He tapped into the religious ethos of his countrymen and used biblical teachings to encourage and embolden his people to stand up to evil and fight for what is good.

Churchill's tactic proved successful as he was able to lead Great Britain to join the Allied Forces and ultimately to defeat the Nazi regime. ■

Panorama of Parliament Square with statue of Winston Churchill, London.

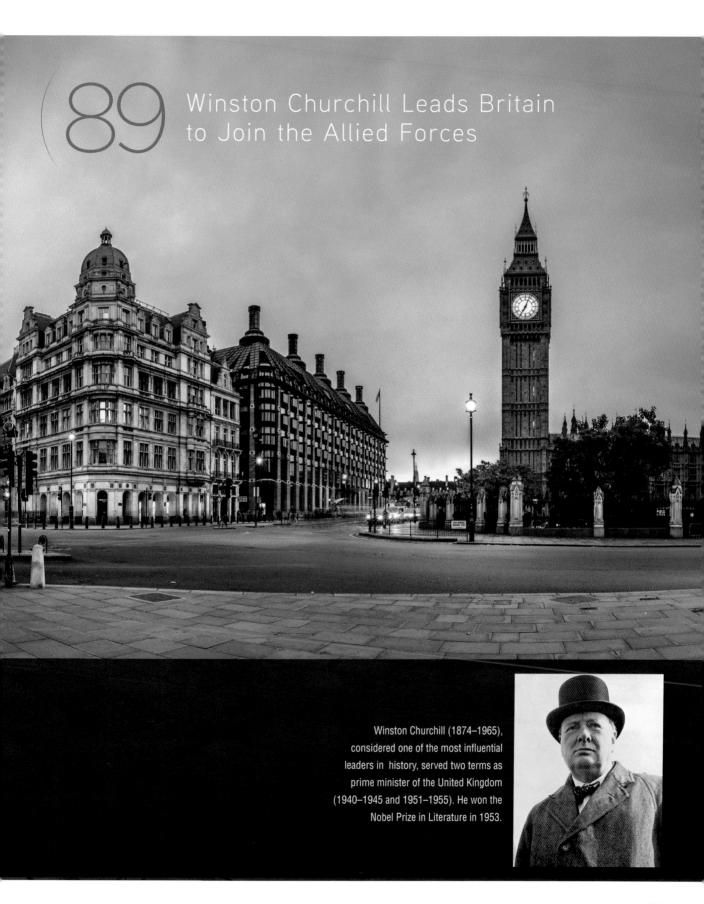

89 Winston Churchill Leads Britain to Join the Allied Forces

Winston Churchill (1874–1965), considered one of the most influential leaders in history, served two terms as prime minister of the United Kingdom (1940–1945 and 1951–1955). He won the Nobel Prize in Literature in 1953.

90 Bedouin Shepherds Discover the Dead Sea Scrolls

In the winter of 1946–1947, three Bedouin shepherds made one of the most important archaeological finds of all time.

The young shepherds found seven ancient scrolls in a cave southeast of Jerusalem and inland from the northwestern shore of the Dead Sea. The scrolls, which were written about 1,000 years before the shepherds found them, reveal valuable information about the Bible and how it came into existence.

After a careful search of other caves in the Qumran area, archaeologists found more than 600 scrolls and thousands of scroll fragments. Fragments of every book of the Bible, except Esther, were discovered, as well as many other texts that shed light on the times in which they were written.

Prior to the discovery of the Dead Sea Scrolls, the oldest existing copies of the Hebrew Bible were two manuscripts from about AD 1000. With the scrolls, however, biblical scholars now are able to compare texts from AD 1000 with versions written in the period from 200 BC to about AD 100.

Of the nearly 200 fragments of the Bible that were found, eighty-seven are from the first five books of the Bible. By studying the fragments, scholars are able to see how much the wording of the Bible has changed over time.

The Dead Sea Scrolls also reveal important information about the historical and cultural context of the writing of the Bible's New Testament. ■

Top: Woman looks at the Dead Sea Scrolls on display at the caves of Qumran.
Left: Qumran caves in Qumran National Park, Israel.

91 Jews Gather in Jerusalem to Celebrate Their First Passover in Modern Israel

On the evening of April 23, 1948, just prior to the declaration of Israeli statehood on May 14 the same year, Jews gathered in Jerusalem with their families to celebrate Passover.

The Jews of 1948 were in the midst of battles with the armed forces of Egypt, Transjordan, Syria, Lebanon, and Iraq. Many people find likenesses in these events to those described by Ezra—the repatriation of exiled Jewish people and the rebuilding of Jerusalem after its destruction by the Babylonians.

In 1948 Jewish citizens of all ages were mobilized to defend Jerusalem. The city had been torn up to block tank attacks, trenches had been dug, and concrete fortifications had been built. A group of 20,000 Arabs fled Haifa two days before Passover.

Tanks delivered meager provisions for the holiday—including fish, potatoes, matzo, dried fruit, and meat—that seemed like a feast to the hungry residents.

Although the fighting continued to rage after that night, the first Passover meal helped forge a new national identity for the people of Israel. ◼

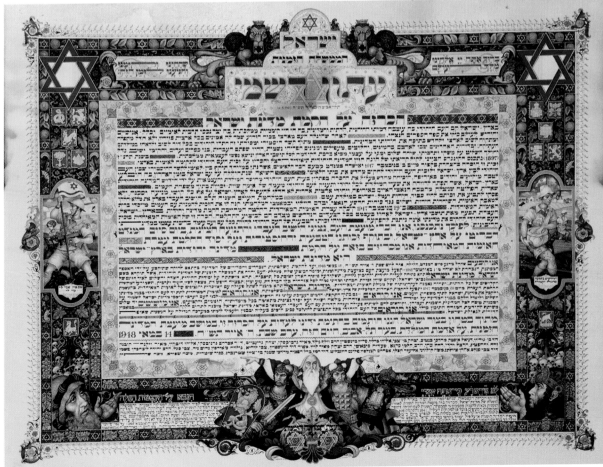

Top: Captain Avraham "Bren" Adan raising the Israeli flag marking the end of the war.
Bottom: Declaration of Independence for the State of Israel, 1948.

92

Mother Teresa Founds the Missionaries of Charity

Mother Teresa of Calcutta was born Gonxha Agnes in Skopje, Macedonia. Her parents were of Albanian descent. Upon adulthood she began training to become a missionary at the Institute of the Blessed Virgin Mary in Ireland. Given the name Sister Mary Teresa, she ventured to Calcutta, India, to teach at a school for girls. It was here that her life and the lives of an immeasurable number of people changed forever.

> *"Being unwanted, unloved, uncared for, forgotten by everybody, I think that is a much greater hunger, a much greater poverty than the person who has nothing to eat."*
>
> *– Mother Teresa*

After a spiritual experience during an annual retreat, Sister Mary returned to India to carry out her new mission to bring love to the unloved—in this case, the poor of Calcutta. Her movement was centered upon care for the indigent. This movement came to span the globe, birthing several other similar organizations to encourage showing love for the poor in many countries. Mother Teresa lived by her words: "By blood, I am Albanian. By citizenship, an Indian. By faith, I am a Catholic nun. As to my calling, I belong to the world. As to my heart, I belong entirely to the Heart of Jesus."[31] ∎

93 Frank País Attempts Overthrow of Batista

ENTRADA A LA HABANA 8 DE ENERO DE 1959

Much of what is written about the Cuban Revolution of the 1950s focuses on Fidel Castro's group of guerrillas in the mountains. However, a large underground movement against General Fulgencio Batista and his use of Cuba's military to seize control of the nation also took place in the urban landscape.

One of the leaders of the underground movement was Frank País. During a time when members of the Communist Party were forming "fighting committees" in Cuba's high schools and universities and influencing the country's professional and business organizations, País began his own group of young revolutionaries.

As a minister's son, País knew that Batista's violent and humiliating tactics used for seizing power opposed the teachings of the Bible. País relied on Proverbs 22:16 ("Whoever oppresses the poor to increase his own wealth, or gives to the rich, will only come to poverty") and other biblical verses to bolster his efforts to overthrow the harsh dictator.

Police officers killed País in the streets of Santiago on July 30, 1957. However, País, who was only twenty-two when he died, left behind a legacy. An estimated 100,000 people flooded the streets of Santiago for his funeral.

Today, the young revolutionary's childhood home is a museum and a national monument, and the international airport in Holguín, Cuba, is named after him. ∎

Above: *Fidel Castro with Rebel Soldiers Entering Havana in 1959* on 1 peso Cuban banknote, 1986.

94 Christian UN Chief Champions the Underdog

In today's vernacular, we often hear the phrase "walk the talk," encouraging us to live out what we believe. Dag Hammarskjöld, a Swedish public servant, who in 1953 became secretary-general of the United Nations, was someone who walked the talk.

During his two terms of service for the UN, Hammarskjöld worked to resolve international conflicts and to protect people viewed as underdogs. For example, Hammarskjöld personally negotiated the release of American soldiers captured by the Chinese during the Korean War, and he is credited with helping to resolve the Suez Canal crisis of 1956. He worked with the UN to prevent the use of force by France, Great Britain, and Israel following Egyptian president Gamal Abdel Nasser's seizure of the Suez Canal for his country.

Both in his diary and in interviews he gave, Hammarskjöld expressed how the Bible had played an influential role in the decisions he made throughout his career. He wrote, "In our era, the road to holiness necessarily passes through the world of action."

In 1961, Hammarskjöld, who received the Nobel Peace Prize posthumously, died in a fiery plane crash while on his way to negotiate a cease-fire in the country today known as the Democratic Republic of the Congo. Some evidence suggests the plane was shot down, but the details of the crash remain a mystery. ■

Top Right: Dag Hammarskjöld, secretary-general of the United Nations (1959).
Above: United Nations, New York.

95

Martin Luther King Jr. Leads Civil Rights Movement

Dr. Martin Luther King Jr. is practically synonymous with the civil rights movement in the United States. Dr. King represented the heart and soul of the movement, and the Bible breathed life into the heart and soul of Dr. King.

A Baptist minister who helped found the Southern Christian Leadership Conference, Dr. King firmly advocated nonviolent civil disobedience as the most effective way to protest segregation and other forms of discrimination experienced by blacks in the American South during the middle of the twentieth century. A fiery and passionate speaker, Dr. King utilized an arsenal of words and his dynamic personality to help organize a series of nonviolent protests, including a bus boycott in Montgomery, Alabama, that was fueled by Rosa Parks's refusal to move to the back of a segregated bus. Moreover, Dr. King also organized the 1963 March on Washington, DC, where he gave his iconic "I Have a Dream" speech. Dr. King was awarded the Nobel Peace Prize in 1964 and was instrumental in the signing of the US Civil Rights Act of 1964—legislation outlawing discrimination based on race, color, religion, sex, or nationality.

Profoundly influenced by the Bible, Dr. King was quick to point out that racial discrimination stands in stark contrast against the teachings of Jesus. "I always go back to Scripture," Dr. King proclaimed one Sunday in a 1966 sermon, "[in order] to find my consolation."[32] Dr. King made frequent use of the Bible, not only in his sermons, but also in his speeches. In doing so, he gave an eloquent voice and a fearless style of leadership to the civil rights movement. He often quoted from Matthew 5:43–48—Jesus's command to love one's enemies—as a way to instill the values of Jesus's teaching into the fight for equality. In his most famous speech, "I Have a Dream," Dr. King quoted directly from Amos 5:24 and Isaiah 40:5, verses that proclaim justice, equality, and peace.

Although he often received death threats, Dr. King was resigned to the danger of his work. In 1968, he was shot and killed while standing on a balcony outside his motel room in Memphis, Tennessee. James Earl Ray, a drifter and former convict, was arrested after an intense two-month manhunt. King's death sparked riots and demonstrations throughout the United States. Nevertheless, it is Dr. King's legacy of peaceful protests and his reliance on his faith in God and on the words of the Bible that continue to inspire people of all races. ■

96

Gary Starkweather Invents the Laser Printer

Gary Starkweather was curious about laser printing. His employer, Xerox, wasn't sure that this revolutionary new idea could be accomplished, but Starkweather felt adamant that he was on to something big and possessed the conviction to pursue it—regardless of dissuasions.

Starkweather believed that humans are made in the image of a creative and innovative God (Genesis 1–2). Many portions of the Bible portray God as the creator of all things, a view of God that motivated Starkweather and perhaps fueled his creativity as he viewed himself as an agent of God's creative abilities. Starkweather considered his act of creating a form of worship. According to him, this mind-set compelled his creative pursuits, which included the laser printer.

Today, the laser printer is arguably one of the most significant inventions of the twentieth century. Its technology has proved invaluable to so many industries around the world. Because of this, it's fascinating to know that its inventor credits God for it all. ∎

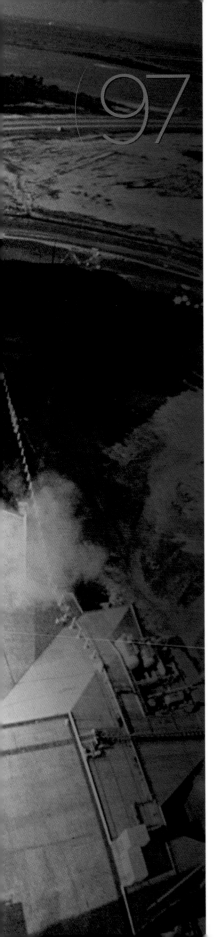

97

Neil Armstrong Walks on the Moon

As spacecraft commander of Apollo 11, the first manned spaceship to the moon, Neil Armstrong was the first person to step on the surface of the moon. His famous words—"One small step for man, one giant leap for mankind"—were broadcast around the world and changed our view of the universe.

Neil Armstrong and fellow astronaut Buzz Aldrin prayed and took communion with a small Bible—brought to the moon by Aldrin—before taking their first steps on the moon. Armstrong also read Bible passages to help him think about what he would say when he made history.

Armstrong returned to earth as a hero. In interviews after he returned from the Apollo 11 mission, Armstrong stated that he felt the presence of God while on the moon. As fellow astronaut John Glenn told reporters after returning from his 1998 space mission, "To look out at this kind of creation and not believe in God is to me impossible."[33] ■

Left: The liftoff of Apollo 11 on a Saturn V missile, July 16, 1969.
Top Right: Neil Armstrong.
Above: Apollo 11 boot print on the moon.

98 Nelson Mandela Negotiates to End Apartheid

South Africa experienced a dark period when the nation embraced apartheid. During this time, thousands of black citizens suffered severe injustice. Because the government was at the root of apartheid, change could only come about by a grassroots effort. Nelson Mandela knew that fighting for the rights of South Africans was the right thing to do. He also understood that it would come at great personal expense.

Nelson Mandela's courage and fortitude in the face of a seemingly hopeless situation was inspired by the accounts of Jesus in the Bible. According to the Gospels, Jesus sacrificed himself to save people, and he expected his followers to willingly give their lives for the sake of others (John 15:13). Mandela sought to prepare himself to fulfill the task of sacrificing his freedom for the justice of the South African people by way of biblical instruction. While Mandela was not outspoken about his religious beliefs, he relied heavily on the teachings of the Bible to get him through the many trials he faced.

The decision to stand up for justice cost Mandela his freedom for many years; he was thrown into prison for his activism. However, Mandela's stand did eventually pay off, and he was ultimately able to secure freedom for many people. ∎

"There can be no greater gift than that of giving one's time and energy to help others without expecting anything in return."
– Nelson Mandela

Above Left: Parts of ghetto in Soweto, a legacy of South African apartheid that can still be seen today.

Above Right: Metal sculpture of Nelson Mandela at the site where he was arrested in 1962 by the apartheid government.

Right: Nelson Mandela smiles as he poses for a portrait during an event in London, May 24, 2006.

99 Paul Rusesabagina Saves Hundreds During the Rwandan Genocide

Paul Rusesabagina, a hotel manager, valiantly worked to save hundreds of people during the Rwandan Genocide of 1994. His story was made famous in the 2004 movie *Hotel Rwanda*.

He frequently referred to the Bible in his autobiography. He cited James 4:14 in his reflections on some of the lessons he learned from his experiences during the genocide:

> I remember reading this in the Bible when I was a young man: "What is your life? You are a mist that appears for a little while and then vanishes" [James 4:14]. Our time here on the earth is short, and our chance to make a difference is tiny. . . . I am a hotel manager, trained to negotiate contracts and provide shelter for those who need it. My job never changed, even in a sea of fire.

> Wherever the killing season should next begin and people should become strangers to their neighbors and themselves, my hope is that there will be those ordinary men who say a quiet no and open the rooms upstairs.[34] ∎

"Come now, you who say, 'Today or tomorrow we will go into such and such a town and spend a year there and trade and make a profit'— yet you do not know what tomorrow will bring. What is your life? For you are a mist that appears for a little time and then vanishes." – James 4:13–14

Top: Ntarama Church altar where 5,000 people seeking refuge were killed by grenade, machete, rifle, and being burnt alive. Photo courtesy of Scott Chacon, Dublin, CA, USA.

References

1. Benjamin Thorpe, *Ancient Laws and Institutes of England* (G.E. Eyre and A. Spottiswoode, printers to the Queen's Most Excellent Majesty, 1840), 55.

2. Barry Hudock, "Summa Theologica: The 'Glory of the Catholic Faith,'" *OSV Newsweekly*, February 10, 2016, https://www.osv.com/OSVNewsweekly/ByIssue/Article/TabId/735/ArtMID/13636/ArticleID/19252/.

3. Gur Zak, *Petrarch's Humanism and Care of the Self* (Cambridge University Press, 2010).

4. *New World Encyclopedia*, s.v. "Peasants' Revolt," accessed May 27, 2017, http://www.newworldencyclopedia.org/entry/Peasants%27_Revolt_(1381).

5. David Zax, "Galileo's Revolutionary Vision Helped Usher In Modern Astronomy," *Smithsonian Magazine*, Smithsonian.com, August 2009, http://www.smithsonianmag.com/science-nature/Galileos-Revolutionary-Vision-Helped-Usher-In-Modern-Astronomy-34545274/.

6. "Galileo Galilei: Misjudged Astronomer," *Christianity Today*, accessed May 27, 2017, http://www.christianitytoday.com/history/people/scholarsandscientists/galileo-galilei.html.

7. "For the Glory of God and Advancement of the Christian Faith," I Took the Red Pill, November 22, 2008, https://itooktheredpill.wordpress.com/2008/11/22/.

8. Ibid.

9. "History and Mission," Harvard Divinity School, Harvard.edu, accessed May 27, 2017, https://hds.harvard.edu/about/history-and-mission.

10. Charles E. Hummel, "Newton's Views on Science and Faith," Christian History Institute, accessed May 27, 2017, https://www.christianhistoryinstitute.org/magazine/article/newtons-views-on-science-and-faith/.

11. "Johann Sebastian Bach: The Fifth Evangelist," Christian History, *Christianity Today*, accessed May 27, 2017, http://www.christianitytoday.com/history/people/musiciansartistsandwriters/johann-sebastian-bach.html.

12. Charles McKenna, "Antoine-Laurent Lavoisier," *The Catholic Encyclopedia*, vol. 9 (New York: Robert Appleton Company, 1910), accessed May 27, 2017, http://www.newadvent.org/cathen/09052a.htm.

13. John Witherspoon, "1776: Witherspoon, Dominion of Providence over the Passions of Men (Sermon)," Online Library of Liberty, accessed August 14, 2016, http://oll.libertyfund.org/pages/1776-witherspoon-dominion-of-providence-over-the-passions-of-men-sermon.

14. Richard Pierard, "William Wilberforce and the Abolition of the Slave Trade: Did You Know?" Christian History, *Christianity Today*, accessed May 27, 2017, http://www.christianitytoday.com/history/issues/issue-53/william-wilberforce-and-abolition-of-slave-trade-did-you.html.

15. Jared Sparks, *The Writings of George Washington*, vol. 12 (Boston: American Stationers' Company, 1837), 407.

16. Michael Faraday, *Matter*, unpublished manuscript, 105.

17. "Departed Saints Yet Living," *The Metropolitan Tabernacle Pulpit Sermons*, vol. 31 (London: Passmore & Alabaster, 1885), 541–542.

18. Georgina Battiscombe, *Shaftesbury: A Biography of the Seventh Earl. 1801–1885* (London: Constable, 1974), 334.

19. Jonathan Bean, ed., *Race and Liberty in America: The Essential Reader* (Lexington: The University Press of Kentucky, 2009), 28–30.

20. George Washington, in a letter dated August 20, 1778, in Jared Sparks, *The Writings of George Washington*, vol. 12 (Boston: American Stationers' Company, John B. Russell, 1837), 402.

21. "William Booth: First General of the Salvation Army," *Christian History*, Christianity Today, accessed May 2017, http://www.christianitytoday.com/history/people/activists/william-booth.html.

22. Marcus Monroe Brown, *A Study of John D. Rockefeller: The Wealthiest Man in the World* (Cleveland, OH: 1905), 45.

23. "Nobel Laureate Guglielmo Marconi: Science Is the Expression of Supreme Will," compiled by Tihomir Dimitrov, 2012 Community, last updated January 4, 2012, http://2012daily.com/community/blogs/browse-by-tag?tag=supreme%20will.

24. Ibid.

25. Amy Carmichael, reading for January 21, *Whispers of His Power: Selections for Daily Reading* (Fort Washington, PA: CLC Publications, 1982).

26. John F. Hutchinson, *Champions of Charity: War and the Rise of the Red Cross* (Boulder, CO: Westview Press, 1996).

27. Albert Schweitzer, "The Apostle Paul: Second of Two Sermons on St. Paul, Sunday 1 June 1930," *The African Sermons*, ed. and trans. Steven E. G. Melamed (New York: Syracuse University Press, 2003), 71.

28. Mary Bagley, "George Washington Carver: Biography, Inventions, and Quotes," Live Science, December 6, 2013, http://www.livescience.com/41780-george-washington-carver.html.

29. Tom Cornell, "A Brief Introduction to the Catholic Worker Movement," The Catholic Worker Movement, accessed May 27, 2017, http://www.catholicworker.org/cornell-history.html.

30. Yukiko Sugihara, *Visas for Life* (Edu-Comm Plus, 1995), 19.

31. "Mother Teresa of Calcutta," Vatican, accessed May 27, 2017, http://www.vatican.va/news_services/liturgy/saints/ns_lit_doc_20031019_madre-teresa_en.html.

32. Dr. Martin Luther King Jr., "Non-Conformist," Sermon, The King Center, January 16, 1966, http://www.thekingcenter.org/archive/document/mlk-sermon-non-conformist.

33. Julie Zauzmer, "In Space, John Glenn Saw the Face of God: 'It Just Strengthens My Faith,'" *Washington Post*, December 8, 2016, https://www.washingtonpost.com/news/acts-of-faith/wp/2016/12/08/in-outer-space-john-glenn-saw-the-face-of-god/?utm_term=.5ddb458174cb.

34. Paul Rusesabagina with Tom Zoellner, *An Ordinary Man: An Autobiography* (New York: Viking Penguin, 2006).

museum of the Bible

Experience the Book that Shapes History

Museum of the Bible is a 430,000-square-foot building located in the heart of Washington, D.C.—just steps from the National Mall and the U.S. Capitol. Displaying artifacts from several collections, the Museum explores the Bible's history, narrative and impact through high-tech exhibits, immersive settings, and interactive experiences. Upon entering, you pass through two massive, bronze gates resembling printing plates from Genesis 1. Beyond the gates, an incredible replica of an ancient artifact containing Psalm 19 hangs behind etched glass panels. Come be inspired by the imagination and innovation used to display thousands of years of biblical history.

Museum of the Bible aims to be the most technologically advanced museum in the world, starting with its unique Digital Guide that allows guests to personalize their museum experience with navigation, customized tours, supplemental visual and audio content, and more.

For more information and to plan your visit, go to museumoftheBible.org.